USE OF FORCE
INVESTIGATIONS:
A Manual for Law Enforcement

USE OF FORCE
INVESTIGATIONS:
A Manual for Law Enforcement

KEVIN R. DAVIS

 RESPONDER™
MEDIA

Responder Media books may be ordered through booksellers or by contacting:

Responder Media
1663 Liberty Drive
Bloomington, IN 47403
www.respondermedia.com
1-(877) 444-0235

ISBN: 978-1-4705-0013-9 (e)
ISBN: 978-1-4705-0012-2 (sc)

Printed in the United States of America

Responder Media rev. date: 9/17/2012

DEDICATION

I would like to dedicate this book to my lovely wife, Patricia. Through good times and bad in a career filled with "interesting times and events" she has had my back. I love her tremendously and she holds my heart.

To my kids – Timothy, Stephanie, Aron and Emily and to my Grandkids – Grant, Tayden and Caston, I'm truly a lucky man.

To my late parents – Bob & Maxine Davis, I won the lottery on parents. There isn't a day that goes by that I don't miss you and your wise counsel.

To my late Uncle Richard Krausman, former Sergeant United States Marine Corps and veteran of Okinawa, his tutelage directed me to my path.

To my "legal" educators on use of force: John Hall (FBI, SAC, ret.), Mike Brave, Laura Scarry, Randy Means, Darrell Ross, Urey Patrick and many, many more, "I stand on the shoulders of giants..." I thank you for your training.

To those police supervisors that I've worked for who have lead from the front and lived the first rule of leadership, "take care of the troops" and actually look out for the brave men and women who work for them. Take heart, your dedication to your troops does not go unnoticed.

To my proofreaders Doug Sandor, Danny Caprez, Chuck Choate, Brian Willis, and Steve Ashley thanks for your time and comments.

Thank you to Brian Willis for the foreword. Your words and instruction have always inspired me and you've set the bar very high on excellence in instruction.

To all my Brothers & Sisters in Blue – especially Chuck Choate, Jack Gilbride, Michael Shaeffer, and Danny Caprez as well as my former teammates on SWAT – thanks for having my back, it was indeed a privilege to serve with you and an honor to train you.

And finally I would like to dedicate this book to our nation's fallen law enforcement officers. To those brave men and women who have paid the ultimate price. I pray that my words, a better understanding of use of force and high quality instruction may reduce future numbers of officers killed in the line of duty.

ADMONISHMENT AND WAIVER

Nothing in this book constitutes legal advice. The author is not an attorney. Readers should consult their own attorneys or police legal advisors for specific legal opinions and research.

Incidents described in this manual are compilations or fictional accounts used to support the subject matter. Any similarity or resemblance to any person living or dead is strictly coincidental.

This manual or guidebook cannot, by the diversity of state laws, be all encompassing. It cannot and should not replace actual training in these vital law enforcement functions. Readers will be provided with suggested articles and books for further study in the "Appendice" section at the end of this manual. Use of force law is fluid and what was once true ten years. ago or last year may not hold true today. Continued study is mandatory.

Further, many of the issues surrounding use of force investigations has contract implications with police unions. Readers should check their labor contracts as well as agency policy and procedure.

This is only a guidebook. The reader agrees to indemnify and hold harmless the author in any legal proceeding resulting from investigations using the material suggested in this book.

CONTENTS

FOREWORD

On the face of it police use of force would appear to be simple:

- Know what you can do.
- Know when you can do it.
- Be prepared to do it immediately.

The sad reality however, is that too many officers do not know what they can do or when they can do it and as a result are not prepared to do it immediately, if at all. This lack of understanding causes officers to hesitate. Hesitation causes officers to be injured and killed every year. This lack of knowledge also results in unlawful or questionable arrests as well as in poorly conducted use of force investigations.

Why do officers not know what to do? Although the answer is multi-faceted the simple response is that they have never been taught. Many officers have been trained in what not to do. They have been taught about the things that will get them sued and get them fired but they have not been trained about what they can do and when they can do it. The inappropriate fear of liability created by many training programs results in officers being afraid to do their jobs and as a result too many officers are injured and killed. Not knowing what to do and when to do it results in officers potentially overreacting or underreacting, both of which are less desirable. Officers have been taught skills and tactics, which are critical, but have not been taught when and how to use the skills and tactics. They have been taught to shoot, fight and drive fast, but not been taught how to think and, they have not been taught how to articulate the reasonableness of their actions.

The people teaching these classes are not evil people out to set up their officers. In many cases they simply do not know themselves so they continue to pass on poor, inaccurate or no information. The problem is compounded when those tasked with conducting use of force investigations have limited, inaccurate or incomplete information on what the law actually allows officers to do and what science tells us about the dynamic nature of use of force events.

It is for these reasons this book, *Use of Force Investigations: A Manual for Law Enforcement,* is so critical to the law enforcement profession. In this comprehensive book renowned law enforcement trainer Kevin Davis lays out the critical elements of use of force for law enforcement trainers, officers and investigators in a methodical and understandable way. Kevin covers the law, provides references and resources, examines actual use of force scenarios and addresses the myths and misconceptions of use of force.

Leadership expert Bill Westfall encourages those in the law enforcement profession to become "Readers, Writers, Thinkers, fighters". Kevin Davis exemplifies the "Reader, Writer, Thinker, fighter" philosophy and uses his skills as a reader, writer and thinker to share his thoughts, knowledge, insights, experience and expertise with the reader so you too can be more than just a fighter. To conduct proper use of force investigations you must be a reader, writer and thinker. You must know what the law says. You must have a working knowledge of policy and procedures and the role they play in use of force events and investigations. You must understand the scientific research regarding the dynamics of tense, uncertain and rapidly evolving events and effects on the human mind and body including the effects of stress on human performance and memory. You must understand the methodology for effectively asking questions to determine the totality of circumstances regarding the use of force event. You must understand the limitations of video and why the video may differ from an officer's memory of what happened. These are all critical elements in determining the reasonableness of the actions of an officer who, through the nature of their job, was thrust by circumstances into the role of 'the fighter'.

Kevin Davis lays all these elements out for you in *Use of Force Investigations: A Manual for Law Enforcement*. This comprehensive works covers critical case law decisions as well as the scientific research you need to know in order to effectively conduct a use of force investigation. He provides you with the case and research citations and references. He provides policy and procedural guidelines and he provides a recommended reading list.

Kevin Davis takes the legal and scientific knowledge, which can be both overwhelming and intimidating and applies it to case studies to help put the theory into practice and make it understandable.

Kevin has a straight forward, no nonsense writing style that is badly needed in the profession. These are critical topics, which can have a significant impact on officers' lives, agency morale and public perception and it is time someone got in the face of our profession to make sure we are doing what is right.

To further quote Bill Westfall he challenges leaders to pass the *Leadership Test* by asking are you doing:

- The right thing
- At the right time
- In the right way
- For the right reason

Use of Force Investigations: A Manual for Law Enforcement is about the Leadership Test as it applies to use of force investigations. In order to do the right ting, at the right time in the right way for the right reason you need to have the right information. *Use of Force Investigations: A Manual for Law Enforcement* gives you the tools to conduct thorough, competent investigations into use of force incidents and pass the Leadership Test.

This is not a book just for use of force investigators. It is a book for law enforcement professions who want to know what they can do and when they can do it so they can mentally prepare to do it immediately. This is a book for law enforcement trainers who want to ensure they are providing their officers with the correct information.

This is not a book to be read and put on a shelf somewhere. This is not a book to be read and passed on to someone else "who really needs to know this". This is a book to be studied. This is a book to be reread. This is a book that cries out for you to underline and highlight important references and citations. This is a book where you have permission to write in the margins. You need to dog-ear the pages of this book to allow you to go back and review critical portions. As you read this book you will think of others who need to read it. Please invest in the profession and get them their own copy so you can keep yours as a personal reference.

Brian Willis
Winning Mind Training
2011 Law Officer Trainer of the Year
ILEETA Deputy Executive Director

CHAPTER 1

UNDER THE MICROSCOPE

Now, like never before, law enforcement use of force is under the microscope. Checking the online police websites just this morning I see that use of force has made national headlines as officers and police actions while moving demonstrators of the "Occupy" crowd out of parks and universities are under scrutiny.

Go to any news website and chances are you'll see a link to the video of a police use of force. Matter-of-fact, oftentimes multiple cell phone camera videos of the same incident will be posted on YouTube the night of an encounter with police.

Talking heads, oftentimes former police chiefs or ex-police investigators, with little knowledge about use of force, will appear on cable news and offer their grandiose opinions while a looped segment of a police use of force plays in the background.

Due to the "politics of force" police agencies are forced to deal with "citizen review boards" and "police auditors" who are usually political appointments with no specialized training.

Special interest groups with traveling "activists" will arrive in a town post use of force incident and make condemning statements about a police agency, its methods, corruption, racial bias and more. With no accountability they ignore the truth and facts of a case to further their agenda.

Even chiefs of police and other department brass, for political reasons or to serve their own career goals and self-interests, will oftentimes throw a good officer under the bus after a shooting, in custody death or use of force captured on video that, "looks bad."

This maelstrom of madness after a use of force incident does not include the seemingly inevitable civil litigation that may arise after a use of force incident.

Nationwide criminal prosecution of officers involved in use of force incidents is on the upswing. Officers are being charged with criminal violations in shootings and other use of force incidents.

Forgotten in all this mess is a lonely and forgotten man or woman in uniform who, with little or no training by his or her agency on use of force, has gotten into a knock down fight for his life with some three time convicted violent criminal. Afraid in the dark or in the light, they were just trying to keep from being assaulted after the academy taught come-along or defensive tactic failed and the suspect just wouldn't let them get his arms behind his back and the fight was on.

And yet valiant hard-working and dedicated male and female officers of all races and ethnic origins put their blue uniforms and duty belts on each day and go out and do "it" every day.

God Bless them!

But we (cities, towns, counties, other government entities and the law enforcement agencies they work for) owe them more. The *more* is that we train officers better in use of force so that they truly understand the legal standards and restrictions of use of force and the major case law involved such as *Graham v. Connor*. We must also attempt to instruct use of force in police basic academies and in-service programs using scenario based training as much as possible. In this way we take the *theory and case histories* out of a static classroom and involve the officer/student more and more realistically so that they see and experience what use of force law is all about to the greatest extent possible. This training must include use of force reporting for it is abundantly true that most officers properly use force but do a terrible job of documenting their actions.

Agencies must also train first-line supervisors and command level personnel in police use of force and the investigative process post incident. It does no good if line officers are well trained in the aspects of use of force and the people that manage and lead them as well as investigate their actions are not. By better understanding use of force law, the physiological, psychological, physical, limitations of memory and more a supervisor is better able to ascertain if the use of force was proper (within the law) or excessive (outside the law).

We do our officers a great disservice by creating hesitancy and trepidation within them for fear of how their use of force will be evaluated. I've heard comments like, "Well they shouldn't punch people because it doesn't look good or the chief doesn't like it." Quite honestly the standard for use of force in this country is not a supervisor or chief's opinion of what looks good or not. These types of statements and "tones" from on-high do a lot of damage to officers making split-second decisions. An officer worrying about *what looks good* on the street can easily get hurt or killed. Although the old "I'd rather be judged by twelve than carried by six," is faulty and simplistic, the notion of an officer being put on trial for excessive use of force in cases where he did the right thing is repugnant to me. As an expert witness I've worked defending too many officers who were charged because the agency and investigating supervisors or internal affairs detectives didn't know what they were doing. This is the antithesis of professional policing and competent internal investigations.

Let us "raise the bar" of training for our officers as well as our supervisors, investigators, administrators in use of force issues.

We are "under the microscope" in police use of force. Let us properly prepare our officers so that they may safely complete their law enforcement mission, properly investigate and discipline them if they use excessive force, support and defend them when they act within the law.

CHAPTER 2

USE OF FORCE LEGAL PARAMETERS

"The case law dealing with the use of force by law enforcement is so deferential to the officers that when they learn of it they are shocked. I can understand why the officer of the street is unaware; there is no excuse for those who supervise them and train them to be unaware. It is even more egregious if they are aware and ignore it"

JOHN HALL (FBI, Special Agent in Charge, ret.)

Several years ago my partner in the Training Bureau and I attended a training session on the legal issues of the use of deadly force. During that course which was mostly attended by chiefs and other assorted high level supervisors from agencies in our state, the instructor gave a hypothetical scenario involving when you could shoot a fleeing felon. Sadly the only two people in the room who knew the answer were my partner and me. Further, and even more disappointing, was the fact that the Tennessee v. Garner decision the question was based on was replicated in a large wall poster at the back of the room. The police attendees simply did not know when you could and could not shoot a violent fleeing felon.

Surprising? Not really. In years since that class I've used my own variation of that scenario in countless use of force investigations and firearm instructor courses I taught for my state peace officers training academy. Amazingly after I taught one class a state instructor in the main campus of the academy was called by a state trooper who had attended. The trooper, actually a supervisor as I remember, told this state instructor that I was improperly teaching use of deadly force law. The academy director quickly dispatched the only attorney on staff at the time to my next course. He reported to his superiors that I was in fact teaching use of force law correctly (and well as a matter of fact). How could a supervisor for a state police agency and one of the main state firearm instructors not know this? Easy, they didn't pay attention in classes they attended and were too wrapped up in *the mechanics of shooting* versus the *when you can and can't shoot.*

Just to prove my point, the reader can give police colleagues the same scenario and ask if/when they would shoot, I'll repeat it here:

"You are on routine patrol..." (This is the old saying repeated before most video simulator scenarios). You've pulled into the local fast food restaurant on a Sunday morning to use the bathroom and get a cup of coffee. As you exit your patrol vehicle you hear a gunshot from inside. Drawing your pistol you put out a shots fired call to dispatch and then advance towards the front doors. As you near the front door you look inside and see a young woman who is obviously dead from a serious gunshot wound to the head. You slowly enter the restaurant when you see a male suspect armed with an AK-47 running behind the counter in the kitchen area. He's moving quickly to the rear. You pursue him on foot as he pushes open the rear exit and runs outside into the parking area. As you exit the rear door you see the suspect who is faster than you running away from the restaurant and then tossing the rifle to the ground. You give a loud warning, "Police, stop or I'll shoot!" The now seemingly unarmed suspect is getting away from you. Can you shoot him?"

A simple hypothetical question but one that, sadly, too many LEO's and supervisors cannot answer.

The answer is yes, you can legally shoot the suspect in the back and not because he may have another gun. It could be that investigators find later that the person shot was actually a restaurant employee who overpowered and disarmed the actual assailant and was running out of fear of being shot. The AK-47 that was thrown to ground may be found later to be a toy. Even with these facts discovered post shooting, the officer still was in compliance with the law at the moment he pulled the trigger. This is based on the SCOTUS (Supreme Court of the United States) in the landmark decision Tennessee v. Garner (1985). The Tennessee v. Garner case ruled that shooting fleeing misdemeanants and non-dangerous fleeing felons violated the Constitution and was unreasonable:

> "The use of deadly force to prevent the escape of all felony suspects, whatever the circumstances, is constitutionally unreasonable. It is not better that all felony suspects die than that they escape. Where the suspect poses no immediate threat to the officer and no threat to others, the harm resulting from failing to apprehend him does not justify the use of deadly force to do so. It is no doubt unfortunate when a suspect who is in sight escapes, but the fact that the police arrive a little late or are a little slower afoot does not always justify killing the suspect. A police officer may not seize an unarmed, nondangerous suspect by shooting him dead."

But the Supreme Court went on to elaborate in the next paragraph:

> "Where the officer has probable cause to believe that the suspect poses a threat of serious physical harm, either to the officer or to others, it is not constitutionally unreasonable to prevent escape by using deadly force. Thus, if the suspect threatens the officer with a weapon or there is probable cause to believe that he has committed a crime involving the infliction or threatened infliction of serious physical harm, deadly force may be used if necessary to prevent escape, and if, where feasible, some warning has been given."

The use of deadly force by law enforcement is a seizure and because of that the Fourth Amendment to the Constitution applies, "The right of the people to be secure in their persons, houses, papers, and effects, against unreasonable searches and seizures, shall not be violated, and no Warrants shall issue, but upon probable cause, supported by Oath or affirmation, and particularly describing the place to be searched, and the persons or things to be seized."

The Garner case was historically significant for abolishing the fleeing felon rule. Prior to this some state laws allowed officers to shoot non-violent fleeing felons. The standard of care of the Fourth Amendment is "Objective Reasonableness."

Such was not always the case. Prior to the Garner case the court had applied the 14th Amendment standard of "due process" in the use of force. The 1973 2nd Circuit case, Johnson v. Glick stated that an officer could use that amount of force that did not "shock the conscience" of the court. A claim of excessive force must examine four factors, they were:

- The need for application of force
- The relationship between the need and the amount of force used
- The extent of injury
- Whether the force was applied in good faith, or maliciously and sadistically

In 1989 SCOTUS arrived at a decision in Graham V. Connor which involved use of non-deadly force by an officer. This case involved use of force on someone, (Dethorne Graham) who was never even arrested. Although I won't reprint the entire case (which can and should be read in its entirety online) I'll hit some highlights. Dethorne Graham was a diabetic who felt the onset of an insulin reaction and sought out his friend William Berry to take him to a convenience store to purchase orange juice. When Graham got to the store he found it was busy and so he hurried out of the store without purchasing anything and asked Berry to drive him to a friend's house. This action led to Officer Connor of the Charlotte, NC Police Department becoming suspicious. Officer Connor performed a traffic stop on Berry's vehicle. Graham, experiencing a low blood sugar reaction, exited the car at one point, ran around it twice and sat down on the curb and briefly passed out. Graham was handcuffed behind his back, lifted up and placed on the hood of Berry's car. Graham regained consciousness and protested that he was a diabetic. At one point he was placed in the rear of a patrol vehicle. Officer Connor checked with the convenience store and ascertained that Graham had done nothing illegal. Graham was never arrested and was released. Subsequently it was found that he had during the incident sustained injuries including a broken foot. Graham sued citing a violation of his civil rights (Title 42 United States Code, Section 1983, alleging that officers had used excessive force in making the stop, in violation of "rights secured to him under the 14th Amendment to the United States Constitution.

The U.S. District Court looked at the Graham case and applied the 14th Amendment and the Johnson v. Glick four part test, i.e. was excessive force applied maliciously and sadistically to cause harm. SCOTUS stated in their decision, "All claims that law enforcement officials have used excessive force – deadly or not 'in the course of an arrest, investigatory stop, or other "seizure" of a free citizen are properly analyzed under the Fourth Amendment's "objective reasonableness" standard."

This was the first time SCOTUS looked at a use of non-deadly force by police. They applied the Fourth Amendment once again and in their decision gave law enforcement important guidelines on use of force. ★Here are some highlights. You are encouraged to read the full decision.

Chief Justice Rehnquist delivered the opinion of the Court:

> "The Fourth Amendment "reasonableness" inquiry is whether the officers' actions are "objectively reasonable" in light of the facts and circumstances confronting them, without regard to their underlying intent or motivation. The "reasonableness of a particular use of force must be judged from the perspective of a reasonable officer on the scene, and its calculus must embody an allowance for the fact that police officers are often forced to make split-second decisions about the amount of force necessary in a particular situation."

> Determining whether the force used to effect a particular seizure is "reasonable" under the Fourth Amendment requires a careful balancing of "the nature and quality of the intrusion on the individual's Fourth Amendment interests" against the countervailing governmental interests at stake."

> The Court cited several cases on this point, "Our Fourth Amendment jurisprudence has long recognized that the right to make an arrest or investigatory stop necessarily carries with it the right to use some degree of physical coercion or threat

thereof to effect it. (Terry v. Ohio). Because, "the test of reasonableness under the Fourth Amendment is not capable of precise definition or mechanical application," (Bell v. Wolfish), however, its proper application requires careful attention to the facts and circumstances of each particular case, including the severity of the crime at issue, whether the suspect poses an immediate threat to the safety of the officers or others, and whether he is actively resisting arrest or attempting to evade arrest by flight."

"The "reasonableness of a particular use of force must be judged from the perspective of a reasonable officer on the scene, rather than with the 20/20 vision of hindsight."

"With respect to a claim of excessive force, the same standard of reasonableness at the moment applies: "Not every push or shove, even if it may later seem unnecessary in the peace of a judge's chambers," violates the Fourth Amendment. The calculus of reasonableness must embody allowance for the fact that police officers are often forced to make split-second judgments – in circumstances that are tense, uncertain, and rapidly evolving – about the amount of force that is necessary in a particular situation."

"As in other Fourth Amendment contexts, however, the "reasonableness" inquiry in an excessive force case is an objective one: the question is whether the officers' actions are "objectively reasonable" in light of the facts and circumstances confronting them, without regard to their underlying intent or motivation."

Recently (2007) SCOTUS applied the Fourth Amendment to police seizure in a pursuit case in Scott v. Harris. Justice Scalia writing the opinion for the majority of the Court stated: Citing (Brower v. County of Inyo), "A Fourth Amendment seizure occurs…when there is a governmental termination of freedom of movement through means intentionally applied." Also, "It is also conceded, by both sides, that a claim of excessive force in the course of making a seizure of the person is properly analyzed

under the Fourth Amendment's 'objective reasonableness' standard."
Citing the Respondent (Harris's attorneys) use of Tenn. v. Garner in
regards to use of "deadly force", Scalia writes, "If so respondent claims
that *Garner* prescribes certain preconditions that must be met before Scott's
actions can survive Fourth Amendment scrutiny: (1) The suspect must
have posed an immediate threat of serious physical harm to the officer or
others; (2) deadly force must have been necessary to present escape, and
(3) where feasible, the officer must have give the suspect some warning."
"Respondent's argument falters at its first step; *Garner* did not establish
a magical on/off switch that triggers rigid preconditions whenever an
officer's actions constitute deadly force. *Garner* was simply an application
of the Fourth Amendment's "reasonableness" test." "Whatever *Garner*
said about the factors that *might have* justified shooting the suspect in that
case, such "preconditions" have scant applicability to this case, which
has vastly different facts." "Although respondent's attempt to craft an
easy-to-apply legal test in the Fourth Amendment context is admirable,
in the end we must still slosh our way through the factbound morass of
"reasonableness."

The Court ruled that Officer Scott's actions did not violate Harris's Fourth
Amendment rights. In doing so the Court reviewed the totality of the
circumstances including the dashboard cameras which recorded the event
(You can watch the pursuit video on YouTube).

The Supreme Court in deciding the Scott case had to "slosh their way
through the factbound morass of reasonableness" and that is what agencies
must do in use of force investigations.

So that is the law as interpreted by the Supreme Court of the United States.
It is not necessarily "easy" to investigate and make a determination if an
officer's use of force violated the "objectively reasonable" standard. That
said, agencies and sadly too many trainers have attempted to simplify this
process and restrict officers in their use of force. I started this legal section
by quoting retired Special Agent John Hall, "The case law dealing with
the use of force by law enforcement is so deferential to the officers that
when they learn of it they are shocked." Despite this agencies still attempt
to restrict their officers via policy. They then set the stage wherein their
own policy is used against them in civil litigation.

Some points are vital here to remember. SCOTUS applied the constitutional standard of the Fourth Amendment to all of these use of force cases. They did not cite state law or agency policy. Matter-of-fact, the courts have been clear that agency policy does not bind like law. *More later on agency policy.

SCOTUS stated that the standard for use of force is objective reasonableness not, "minimum use of force" or "only that amount of force which is necessary." Matter-of-fact it is entirely possible that in "situations that are tense, uncertain and rapidly evolving and totality of the facts and circumstances" an officer's shooting of a suspect who pointed what is later found to be a cell phone, may be reasonable. Since we are not to engage in "20/20 hindsight" information learned after is irrelevant, "Not every push or shove, even if it may later seem unnecessary in the peace of a judge's chambers, violates the Fourth Amendment." I once testified as an expert in defense of a police sergeant who was charged with Felonious Assault in a use of force incident. As part of my testimony I referred to this section. The prosecutor on cross examination handed me the Graham v. Connor decision and asked something like, "Well Mr. Expert Witness…here's the Supreme Court decision in Graham V. Connor. Can you show me where it says that?" Reviewing the Graham paperwork he handed me, I found this section and quoted it to the jury the prosecutor quickly grabbed the case paperwork away from me and said, "That's not what that means…" I looked at the jury and asked, "Do you want me to read it again?" The officer was acquitted.

In the Graham decision the court stated that the test of reasonableness is, "not capable of precise definition or mechanical application." This means that there is no single answer to a use of force examination. The officer could have possibly used joint locks, pepper spray, the Taser, a knee strike or verbal direction in the same incident and each one could have been reasonable. Further, based on the facts and circumstances, *all of the foregoing use of force could have been used by one officer or multiple officers* and still be reasonable.

It is the role of the police supervisor or investigator to gather the, "facts and circumstances of each particular case, including the severity of the crime at issue, whether the suspect poses an immediate threat to the safety of the officers or others, and whether he is actively resisting arrest or attempting to evade arrest by flight." The investigating supervisor or detective is the means by which all of this information and material is gathered and recorded.

When investigating and coming to a conclusion on an officer's use of force, the question is, at the moment the officer used the force, was it objectively reasonable? That is sometimes a job that requires careful analysis of the totality of the circumstances. The facts and circumstances must be developed by the investigator using: a proper written report of the facts as remembered by each officer involved; oral interviews of suspects & witnesses; review of all videos available; physical environment including lighting and distance; any forensic or ballistic evidence gathered, and more including the physiological effects of fight or flight on the officer and limitations of his memory.

★Readers are strongly encouraged to pick-up a copy of the 2nd edition of *In Defense of Self and Others…": Issues, Facts & Fallacies – the Realities of Law Enforcement's Use of Deadly Force;* by Urey Patrick and John Hall (2010; Carolina Academic Press) for a better understanding of the legal parameters of deadly and non-deadly force.

CHAPTER 3

TEACHING USE OF FORCE

Attorney Randy Means uses a verbal scenario to ask the determination of which use of force action or instrument is objectively reasonable. I'll attempt to use his scenario (as best as I can remember it):

"You are on routine patrol..." (okay, that's mine, here's Randy's): You are working uniform patrol on the nightshift. It is 2300 Hrs. You observe a suspect with a confirmed warrant for Failure to Appear on a Misdemeanor case in the downtown area. He runs away from you down an alleyway. You give chase on foot. The suspect comes to a chain link fence blocking his way. He grabs hold of the fence as you approach. You tell him "You are under arrest for a Misd. warrant. Let go of the fence and put your hands behind your back!" He/she refuses. The suspect is your sex, size and weight. Is it a reasonable use of force to do one of the following? Can you reach out and attempt to forcibly remove his hands from the fence? Can you reach out stabilize his head and using the pressure point below his ear above his jaw (Mandibular Angle) apply finger-tip pressure while giving loud, repetitive verbal commands to let go and submit to arrest? Okay, could you, as an alternative, grab his left wrist and deliver a hammer-fist to the mound of his left forearm (motor point strike to the radial nerve)? How about a knee strike to the outside of his left thigh? Could you grab your pepper spray and spray him in the face to get him to let go of the fence? How about drawing your Taser, removing the cartridge and giving the suspect a drive stun to the left thigh/buttock area to get him to let go? Could you draw your Taser step back several feet and fire the probes at his back? OK, could

you after advising the suspect he is under arrest and his refusal to let go, draw and load your ASP baton and deliver a baton strike to his right thigh? After the suspect (who is your same sex, size and weight) refuses to submit to arrest could you get your baton out and strike him in the head? Finally, could you draw your pistol and shoot a suspect, wanted for a Misdemeanor warrant who won't let go of the fence, in the back of the head?

Now let's make clear that the last two use of force questions in the scenario – *intentionally hitting the suspect in the head with a baton and certainly shooting a non-violent suspect in the head may be excessive uses of force.* Let me reiterate that striking a suspect in the head with a baton and especially shooting a non-violent Misdemeanor warrant suspect *is excessive in this scenario.* ★It may be reasonable, however, when dealing with a fleeing violent felony suspect however based on the totality of the circumstances.

Oftentimes police officers are criticized for not exhausting all other options or for using less-intrusive means in a use of force, i.e. "He didn't have to shoot and kill the knife armed suspect, he could have - shot him in the leg, used a Taser or tackled him." In Plakas v. Drinski the Seventh Circuit Court of Appeals noted, "There is no precedent in this circuit (or any other) which says that the Constitution requires law enforcement officers to use all feasible alternatives to avoid a situation where deadly force can justifiably be used. There are, however, cases which support the assertion that, where deadly force is otherwise justified under the Constitution, there is no constitutional duty to use nondeadly alternatives first."

What we have determined is that as the Supreme Court noted in Graham, the test of reasonableness is not capable of precise definition. What we have instead is, as my friend and noted Federal Law Enforcement Training Center instructor John Bostain has said is, a "range of reasonableness."

Unfortunately, agencies and trainers have attempted to simplify the training and evaluation of police use of force through things called "continuums" or matrixes.

To begin with these continuums had laudable goals, to help: 1. Teach use of force, and 2. Evaluate use of force. The problem was that some trainers began to use these devices as a means to make money. After developing a force continuum they sold their courses to law enforcement ($500 for a one day, eight hour program) and then they sold their services as expert witnesses, "I'd gladly help your agency out using my spiffy multi-colored, survey based continuum," Mastercard® and Visa® are accepted. I've had these "expert witnesses" state such things as, "You don't want to train with company "A", I'm more available for expert witness work," and the like. I'm not against the free market or people making money but when state academy employees pursue this angle I find it a little questionable.

Further, these continuums are the mechanical devices which the Supreme Court proscribed against using in the Graham decision. To quote Thomas Petrowski, FBI SAC and attorney (October, 2002; FBI Bulletin), "Unfortunately, many law enforcement agencies have adopted training in the guise of a "force continuum," which is precisely the mechanical application that the Court proscribed...it is inconsistent with the concept of reasonableness. Most use-of-force continua indicate a reflective approach to a menu of force options with the goal of selecting the least intrusive option. While virtually every force continuum provides that such progressing through force options may not be appropriate in all use-of-force situations, the seed of hesitation is inescapably planted. The word *continuum* implies a sequential approach. The goal of force continua – using the least intrusive means to respond to a threat – simply is not constitutionally required. The law does not require officers to select the minimum force necessary, only a reasonable option."

Some purveyors of these continuums go further by not actually referring to use of force as...use of force. Now what the reader should understand is that the term Confrontational Continuum® has been copyrighted by Kevin Parsons, PhD which means that others have had to change their continuums to reflect this registered copyright. This has led to a variety of continua names in the business. Some have changed *and copyrighted as well* their continua even calling them such things as Response to Suspect's Actions or similar. Let us be clear, as John Bostain from the Federal Law Enforcement Training Center has so adamantly pointed out, force is proactive or preemptive in nature; it is not responsive. We don't use force for what a suspect has done, we use force to keep a suspect from violently acting, resisting or attacking. For instance, we need not wait for a suspect to attack to use force to control. Waiting for the punch, kick, spit or gunshot to come means that we are behind the reactionary curve and it is entirely possible we will be hit, kicked, spat upon or even shot if we wait. Enough research has been done on response time (the combination of the mental process "reaction time" and "movement time" defined as the start to finish of the responder's action) to prove that a person with a gun in his hand presents a deadly threat to an officer because he can shoot before that officer can even raise his pistol from a ready position and fire. Even though such terminology and even the "research" that has supposedly gone into a continuum's development, no matter how pretty they are in color or design. No matter if, like a game show, "the survey says…" 100 people said you could do "B" if a suspect did "A" – they are still the antithesis of what SCOTUS said in Graham.

Further as eminent police attorney Laura Scarry has stated, agencies that use continuums in training let alone policy, frequently are forced to make motions to exclude these same devices in use of force litigation because it will be used against them. I am familiar with one such agency that removed the continuum from their policy but kept using it as a training aid. In a use of force case that resulted in a death of one of their inmates, this came back to haunt them.

It's funny that the manufacturers of these continuums come up with ways in which the "steps" or "levels" should be disregarded based on such things as: officer / subject size, skill level, injury, exhaustion, etc. It is as if they acknowledge that making an arrest or taking a person into custody is not an exact science or process and that as the court noted reasonable force is not capable of precise definition or mechanical application and yet, they persist (mostly to make a buck in my opinion).

It is therefore in my professional opinion that continuums should be avoided.

Let me end this section on continuums by reporting a use of force that recently happened in my area. *On a fall Saturday afternoon, an officer in uniform responded to a 911 call from a female motorist who stated a male suspect had just kicked her car. When the officer pulled up he tried verbal persuasion techniques to no avail and was verbally assaulted by the male in his 50's. At 5 feet 9 inches and 190 lbs. the officer did not fear the older male who was 5'10" and 175 lbs., as the officer approached the suspect. The officer attempted to "escort" the man back to his patrol unit but was quickly assaulted by the suspect who turned and punched the officer in the face. The blow connecting to the officer's jaw rocked him. Drawing his Taser the officer fired, with both probes connecting the suspect in the chest. The suspect reacted by looking down at the probes and stating, "It's on!" A second punch by the suspect broke the officer's nose. Expanding his tactical baton the officer began swinging and connecting with the suspect's head and face. After 12 to 15 strikes with the baton the suspect was unfazed and the officer thought he might have to shoot the guy. Before the officer could draw his pistol, the suspect connects with a punch to the officer's mouth. Dazed and confused the officer is then assaulted by the suspect who picks him up and slams him to the ground. The suspect pinned the officer's arm to the ground, takes the expandable baton and begins beating the officer with the baton. It was only the actions of a former Marine bystander who at 6'2" and 280 lbs. grabbed the suspect from behind and took him to the ground, which saved the officer.*

(Canton Repository, 12/12/2011)

How can such an incident, like so many law enforcement officers face on the street be neatly categorized by a continuum? How does the committed intent and mental drive by a seriously violent suspect factor into using such a continuum? Policing on the streets is substantially different than gymnasiums and offices where tactics, techniques and theoretical concepts like continua *seem reasonable*. It is only when these "artificial contrivances" are subjected to the realities of a determined violent offender that they fall apart. We do our officers a disservice by burdening them down with concepts such as continuums which are largely based on the idea of using the *minimum* amount of force to avoid civil litigation versus the legal standard of *a range of objectively reasonable force*.

As I was finishing this manual I happened upon a new book by a veteran LE trainer and very active expert witness. I had high hopes for the book (which is mostly about use of force and civil litigation) based on the chapter on standards governing the use of force. The author did a good job of covering Tenn. v. Garner and Graham and much of the law as I have done. However, I think things go south when he advocates the use of a continuum (to be sure not just *any continuum* but the one he devised after finding fault in most other designs) for use in training officers in basic and in-service training. He cites the ease of the continuum as a device to accomplish that goal. Though he acknowledges that most officers cannot fairly articulate their continuum under legal examination, he still advocates agencies use one? One of the prerequisites for a continuum, according to the author, is that it must be easily understood; by both the new cadet in the academy as well as the layman juror who will be exposed to it in court. The problem I have with this particular continuum are the terms such as: **static**, **active** and **ominous resistance**. Although they are in most officers' vocabulary, the author's definition is possibly something else. For instance, the author uses the term "static" instead of "passive" as is commonly used to describe someone resisting by sitting or lying down and not moving. Although static may relate to their lack of movement, the resistor employing this tactic is still active. The suspect who grabs onto a steering wheel or park bench can hardly be referred to as "static" as they are once again actively resisting. The author's use of the word "ominous" is interesting as well. Used to describe threatened attacks as well as actual strikes, kicks and the like, the **ominous** category requires explanation by the author and still connotes **active resistance.**

Absent from this continuum are the special circumstances and officer/subject factors so often used by these matrix purveyors. The pigeon-holing that **is** the continuum, e.g. (if he shoves you attempting to escape, you can: use pressure points, joint locks, takedowns, empty hand striking, but not spray him with OC, Taser him or use your baton) you get a waiver from, if: the suspect is a male and the officer is a female; the officer is older than the suspect; the officer is exhausted or is injured; or if the officer is bigger and stronger than the suspect; or it's Tuesday. I inserted the Tuesday part but these matrix methods are designed to try to make order out of chaos and are simply not conducive to describing the anarchy or out of control nature of police/suspect encounters on the street.

For instance, the notion that a larger/stronger officer must limit his use of force on the street against females or smaller males sets the stage for an officer holding back and subsequently being assaulted by an actively resisting suspect regardless of height and weight or gender. Any officer with street experience can relate a story about himself or another officer being scratched to pieces by a petite female or picked up and tossed by a suspect on PCP, Bath Salts or an EDP (Emotionally Disturbed Person) off their meds. How about the big, strong and well-trained officer who gets sucker punched or is inattentive and caught off guard? Are they restricted by their size from defending themselves when faced with an active or **ominous** resisting suspect? The truth is that just like every other use of force incident, the actions of the suspect must be explained as well as the totality of the circumstances and the force must be articulated and justified by the officer and then investigated by a supervisor with the officer's force either approved or disapproved.

Refreshing is a statement by the author in the policy section recommendations of the book which suggests that continuums should not become part of official policy and that agencies stick to Tenn. v. Garner and Graham v. Connor when formulating their use of force policy. Inconsistent, you be the judge?

Most of these types of tools are hardly a **blueprint** for use of force by officers. They become overly restrictive and confusing because of all the definitions, exceptions, factors and circumstances. They become a **map** that does not indicate **the route to get there from here** or **the way you've traveled.** They are the tools the plaintiff's attorneys will use against you to intimate that you strayed from the path that your agency has clearly laid out and are outside the parameters of force that the graph, matrix or continuum allows.

How then do we determine reasonableness without using a continuum? Howard Rahtz writes in *Understanding Police Use of Force* (2003, Criminal Justice Press), "Certainly, reasonable officers may disagree about the constitutional 'reasonableness' of police action in various cases. Thus, in expounding on the notion put forth in the *Graham* case that 'objective reasonableness' is not subject to precise definition, the court in *Malley v. Briggs* (1986) said: 'The objective reasonableness test is met if officers of reasonable competence could disagree on the legality of the defendant's action." Objectively "unreasonable" uses of force would then have reasonably competent and well-trained officers in complete agreement that the force used was excessive.

How to teach use of force then? First and foremost the constitutional parameters of use of force must be taught. Then verbal scenarios like the one I borrowed from Randy Means must be given. Labs or scenarios involving role-players are the next progression with the student actually thrust into non-deadly and deadly force scenarios including Terry stops based on reasonable suspicion up to crimes in progress and then requiring those students to complete use of force reports documenting their actions. This progression of static classroom learning through scenarios incorporates more of the learning modalities – auditory, visual and kinesthetic.

> "I hear and I forget. I see and I remember.
> I do and I understand." – Confucius

Basic academy training must be followed up by in-service training on a regular basis. It is simply not effective to teach the physio-motor skills of suspect control or defensive tactics and shooting and not incorporate the legal parameters of use of force. Further, investigators or front-line supervisors should have specialty training on the process of the use of force investigation and determination of reasonableness as well as other issues relating to specialty investigations like police involved shootings.

We as agencies, trainers and supervisors must, as much as possible, clarify in our officer's mind when they can and can't use force to detain, arrest or other situation such as involuntary mental commitment.

> "We must avoid substituting our personal notions of proper police procedures for the instantaneous decision of the officer at the scene. We must never allow the theoretical, sanitized world of our imagination to replace the dangerous and complex world that policeman face every day."
> (Smith v. Freeland, 6th Circuit Court, 1992)

CHAPTER 4

AGENCY POLICY

Policy sets the stage, details the process and educates the officer about the parameters of the use of deadly and non-deadly force. Policy and procedures are required reading by agency members and the standard to which they will be held accountable, policy should be: regularly reviewed; prioritized from those police activities that have high frequency and high criticality to actions that aren't performed regularly and don't have a high potential for injury, civil rights violation and liability.

Having been present during policy review and cited as "officer most knowledgeable" on several use of force related policies, I can attest to the quagmire that policy review committees sometimes turn into. Pet issues can really bog down the process. The old, "I read an article," or "I went to a class and they said…" can really throw a monkey-wrench in the process. That said my belief over the years has changed from an "all-inclusive" view of use of force policy to a guideline view.

Further as need has arisen I have seen multiple use of force policies developed. For instance, I like a general use of force policy that details when an officer can and can't use deadly or non-deadly force and that further indicates what the reporting and investigation process post incident are. I then like separate policies for non-deadly weapons systems such as Oleoresin Capsicum (pepper spray) and ECD's (Electronic Control Devices, i.e. the Taser). I am also very partial, based on abuses and problems in the past, of an "Officer Involved Death or Serious Bodily Harm" policy which indicates the process an officer involved in a shooting or other incident will go through and the steps the agency will take in these investigations. *The Officer Involved Death or Serious Bodily Harm" policy is better than an officer involved "shots fired" policy because it includes death of a suspect in custody and other incidents such as a pursuit which ends in the death of a suspect.

What happens when an officer violates departmental policy? Well, she can be disciplined with everything from a verbal reprimand up to and including termination. What happens when an agency violates its own policy? Nothing happens. At least no punitive actions, agencies can routinely violate their own policies.

That's not to say that there isn't a fall-out for an agency violating its own policy. It will certainly not look good in arbitrator's hearings or in civil court if the agency violated its own policy. Imagine an agency (supervisors) conducting a use of force investigation without a thorough understanding or application of its own policy. They conclude that an officer used excessive force and then terminate the officer only to be determined later that the use of force was not only within the range of reasonableness but also within policy. What happens then? Oops, we're sorry?

I worked on a case as an expert witness for the defense team where an officer was charged with two counts of misdemeanor assault. The officer had responded to a call of a large fight with possible gunshots. Prior to entering the parking area of the park where the incident was taking place, a vehicle occupied by four suspects fleeing the area hit the officer's patrol vehicle at a speed sufficient to drive him into the opposite lane and deploy the airbags. The officer, who was not wearing his seatbelt at the time because he had jumped into his car in the parking lot of the substation up the street and not put his belt on, hit the windshield, the airbag and the dash area. Both arms were injured to the point of later surgery to repair his right (gun-side) arm tendons. After being injured by the impact (unknown to him if he was intentionally rammed or whether the suspects were armed) he drew his duty pistol and ordered the occupants to show their hands and get out of the car. When they refused, although injured and by himself despite other LEO's in close proximity who were not providing back-up, he removed the driver and the other occupants by force (kicking them in the legs). All of the officer's kicks stopped after they complied except for one kick to one suspect. The rear driver's side passenger suspect was on the ground after he rounded the back of the car and the officer thought this suspect, was the driver attempting to move away from where he had placed him.

Despite two high level supervisors being told the night of the incident by the officer that he had used force on all four suspects, contrary to their policy no use of force investigation was initiated. Further at no time prior to this officer being placed on trial for two counts of assault, did the agency ever interview him (also a violation of their policy). When an investigation was commenced several weeks later, the supervisor conducting it cloaked his mission by telling the suspects he interviewed that he was investigating the traffic crash. In their outdated (by their own training bureau statements) policy it called for a "use of force committee" to meet on the incident and render a written opinion. This was violated as well. Despite the many and numerous times this agency and its investigator violated policy they still charged their own man with crimes he did not commit. At trial when I testified all of these facts came out. They certainly didn't look good and fortunately the officer was acquitted. Refusing to admit that his agency and his supervisors had botched the investigation and not followed their own policy the chief retaliated against me. It took threats of a First Amendment civil suit from my attorney to stop the retaliation.

So what good was this agency's policy? No good at all because it was excessively wordy, outdated, contained the language of a continuum (remember that same type of device that the Supreme Court's Graham decision cautioned against?). That's right; those wall charts that were originally supposed to only be a training tool have been incorporated into agency policy. The result is a "menu" of force options, i.e. if the suspect pulls away, an officer can knee strike them to the motor points of the leg and everything "lesser" on the chart." Attempting to organize chaos these continuum based policies are more restrictive than the law.

Now that's not to say that an agency cannot be more restrictive than the "objective reasonableness" standard. It's just that by doing so an agency sets the stage where their officer's use of force may be perfectly legal but violate policy. This has never made sense to me. For instance some agencies restrict their officers from firing at or from a moving vehicle. In my opinion and attorneys I've dealt closely with in defending officers, this is a mistake. Certainly an officer has the right to fire in defense of his life or the life of another when he believes his life or the life of another is being threatened with death or serious bodily harm. Agencies through training would like the officer to understand that shooting a driver dead creates an unguided missile capable of striking anyone in its path or that vehicles are not homogenous in their design and a bullet that may go through a windshield may career off a piece of metal around it striking an innocent third party. By the way, courts have ruled that although there is certainly liability for striking an innocent third party, you cannot accidentally seize someone, so the Fourth Amendment and its "objective reasonableness" test does not apply to innocent persons who are struck accidentally with police bullets.

Are we really not using policy in this case to attempt to solve what is a training issue? Is this not oftentimes the case? Rather than invest the time in training the officer when to shoot/not shoot we make overly restrictive policies.

As an example, many agencies include in their policy requirements for the use of deadly force the following:

> Intent
> Ability
> Opportunity
> Preclusion

The policy states that before an officer can use deadly force, the suspect must have the intent, ability and opportunity to cause death or serious bodily harm to the officer or others and the officer has precluded all lesser force options. Balderdash! I debated the non-police author of an on-line article on a major police website requiring this tripe before an officer shot a suspect. The author's premise was that police shoot too many people they shouldn't and that by requiring these standards it would reduce these unnecessary shootings. My response was that it may be the cause of many police officers getting killed in the line of duty as well! This is unacceptable when you consider that there are vastly more suspects that an officers *could have shot and didn't each year* than those who were.

Requiring officers to somehow *mind read a suspect's intent* when he is armed with a gun prior to shooting him is not required by law and builds in an unacceptable mental lag time. I recommended the writer of the article read Urey Patrick and John Hall's book, *In Defense of Self and Others...* as I have already recommended to you.

Why make your policy more complicated and restrictive than the law? I believe the answer is in attempts to micromanage officer's actions and to attempt to reduce liability. An advocate of more restrictive policies has stated, "It is up to the executive whether officers are directed to use "minimum force" or "reasonable force." Really, I thought the case-law was pretty clear. In Smith v. Freeland, the court stated, "The issue is whether the officer violated the Constitution, not whether he should be disciplined by the local police force." The notion here is that more restrictive is good and will reduce the likelihood of excessive force incidents. Sadly the detailed and extensive policy creates tentativeness in officers. SCOTUS in the Terry v. Ohio decision stated, "It would be unreasonable to require that officers take unnecessary risks in the performance of their duties." The end result may be that officer's use less force in the beginning stages of an encounter because they are unsure of what they can or can't do. This can lead to situations escalating out of control to the point where more force is now necessary.

> "Requiring officers to find and choose the least intrusive alternative would require them to exercise superhuman judgment. Imposing such a requirement would inevitably induce tentativeness by officers, and thus deter police from protecting the public and themselves."
>
> (Scott v. Heinrich, 9th Circuit, 1994)

The more restrictive policy creates a conundrum and creates two standards the officer is held accountable to: the legal standard and policy. Since most agencies in use of deadly and non-deadly force investigations really don't conduct two separate investigations, rather relying on the findings of the criminal investigation to supply facts for the internal investigation, two standards magnifies your work, i.e. he had a legal use of force but now he has to be disciplined. This can certainly increase liability and be used against an agency.

In the 1990's the FBI began contemplating a change in their use of deadly force policy. As recounted in the book *Deadly Force: What We Know* (William Geller, Michael Scott; Police Executive Research Forum; 1992:

"There is, however, an emerging counter-trend that deserves note. This trend is to pull back from a defense-of-life posture to one that adheres strictly to only those obligations imposed by Tennessee v. Garner."

"At the permissive extreme, the Court's language would support as legitimate a shooting of a *currently non*violent, *fleeing* suspect whom the officer reasonably believes committed a felony involving the *threat* but *not* the *use* of force."

"If such a shooting would violate the *spirit* of the *Garner* ruling, it would not seem to violate the *letter* of the decision."

"No responsible friend or foe of the police today suggests that local police agencies would, as a matter of *policy*, encourage shootings that violated the constitutional requirements of *Tennessee v. Garner*, which FBI sources believe are still less stringent than the Bureau's proposed policy in some ways. Rather, the concern, as noted above, is that, in *practice*, ill-trained, incompetent, or malevolent officers will make more mistakes or hide more of their misdeeds in the aftermath of a department policy relaxation that would be possible under a defense-of-life standard. Police Foundation President Hubert Williams' reaction to the FBI's intention to modify its policy exemplified the perceptions of many in the police profession: "If you provide that level of discretion in police departments, I think there will be more abuses and more instances of people shot by police. (*Law Enforcement News* 1990)."

It is discouraging to hear comments such as "in *practice*, ill-trained, incompetent, or malevolent officers will make more mistakes or hide more of their misdeeds in the aftermath of a department policy relaxation…" as if policy could restrain or prevent tragedies from – ill-trained, incompetent, or malevolent officers? Further, are we to restrict officers from using the full discretion of the law to protect their very lives?

I would say that twenty years after the FBI changed its policy and accepted the *Tenn. v. Garner* standards for use of deadly force against fleeing felons, we have not had an upsurge in shootings of fleeing felons or suspects killed by police. Matter-of-fact, the number of suspects killed by police has pretty much stayed the same as we'll cover in the Officer Use of Deadly Force Investigations section of Chapter 7.

It is interesting to note that the authors mention Tennessee v. Garner and the Supreme Court's decision in the use of deadly force in such a negative manner as if stating that it is a bad thing for officers to follow the law? Further, despite *Deadly Force: What We Know* being published in 1992, *Graham v. Connor* appears nowhere in the text?

As a final note on this subject, nationally known law enforcement risk management expert and trainer Steve Ashley has stated that by focusing on reducing liability as the driving force of law enforcement training for ten or more years we did not reduce officers killed or assaulted. By focusing on proper training of LE personnel and giving them realistic policies on use of force and training them properly in deadly and non-deadly force skills we have a win/win situation: 1) The officer wins the day against the suspect, and 2) We reduce liability. Proper focus here is vital!

Why not have *congruence* between policy and the law? In other words, why not have a policy that is based on the legal precedents of Garner and Graham? It is in this area that agencies hurt themselves by including statements such as, "Officers will only use the minimum amount of force which is necessary to control a suspect." A seemingly laudable goal an officer is not limited by law to the "minimum amount of force" but rather a "range of reasonableness" including several different options and tools based on the totality of the circumstances. All the force may in fact be found to be unnecessary in the end. As an example, officers have shot and killed suspects armed with all manner of innocuous non-deadly items such as cell phones, wallets, combs, etc. but "at the moment" the officer pulled the trigger, the deadly force used was determined to be based on reasonable perceptions and totality of the circumstances which were found to be objectively reasonable. Now, officers in these situations may be facing a subject intent on "suicide by cop" (using the police to cause their death by wielding the item in such a way and making threatening movements or motions, such that a reasonable officer would fear his death) or it could be the lighting was such that the officer perceived the worse because time and conditions prevented them from making a proper identification.

Does policy have to be all inclusive? Absolutely not and this is an impossible goal to accomplish regardless. Sadly agencies which insist on following certain certification standards are almost guaranteed of a more restrictive and excessively wordy use of force policy. I have seen policies which do an adequate job of incorporating both. As an excellent reference I would refer the reader to the writings of attorney Mike Brave from LAAW International, Inc. which are available on-line at www.laaw.com. I would recommend that agencies have several different use-of-force related policies. First of all a general policy that explains the parameters of the use of deadly and non-deadly force, this policy would include Tennessee v. Garner elements in the use of deadly force to apprehend fleeing felons. It would also include elements of Graham v. Connor. This basic policy would state as its foundation, "Officers may use that amount of force which is objectively reasonable based on totality of the circumstances." Further, points from the Graham decision should be included, i.e.: proper application requires careful attention to the facts and circumstances of each particular case, including the severity of the crime at issue, whether the suspect poses an immediate threat to the safety of the officers or others, and whether he is actively resisting arrest or attempting to evade arrest by flight. This general policy need not include items such as what firearms and ammunition are carried, firearm qualification issues and the like which are better served in Chief's Orders or Training Bulletins. The idea is to minimize the use of force policy to increase understanding and implementation by limiting it to the most important relevant topics. Cover less important issues and topics in other policies or through other means.

POST USE OF FORCE POLICY CONTENTS

After the legal aspects of deadly and non-deadly force are covered in the policy, it must contain sections on officer and supervisor responsibilities and reporting procedures. Now it is important for an agency to *define use of force*. What does this mean? Well "technically" a use of force could be construed by some as any application of force. So if an officer grabs the arm of a suspect to keep him from walking away or must forcibly (light physical force) move a suspect's arm behind his back to handcuff, some agencies would require a force report. Under these circumstances and by initiating this requirement an active agency could "bury" itself in paperwork. Patrol officers and supervisors wouldn't be able to patrol or supervise because they would be so busy in the station typing.

At the other end are those agencies that only investigate use of force incidents where the suspect is injured. To emphasize, I believe this is a huge error. So the question is what are the parameters of a use of force which require reporting and investigation? I believe the following are good guidelines:

Officers Responsibilities:

1. Immediately notify his supervisor:
    a. After striking, kicking, tackling a subject, using chemical defense spray, electronic control device, or a K-9 (bite).
    b. Of any injury or alleged injury to officers or civilians.
    c. Of any damage to police or civilian property.
    d. When the subject is charged with resisting arrest.
    e. Any time the officer feels it necessary.
    f. If it is not practical to call a supervisor to the scene, the officer involved in the incident shall contact a supervisor as soon as possible following the incident.
    g. In the case of an off duty incident, and the officer is unsure if the incident involved police employment or actions under the color of law, the officer shall notify a supervisor.

Yes, it is entirely possible that an officer can take a person down to a grassy lawn without striking them and not do a use of force report but it is more probable that a suspect claims injury from some innocuous action by the officer such as grabbing an arm and escorting them away from an incident. Even though there is no visible physical injury, we must report and investigate to protect ourselves and the agency. We must advocate that officers notify their supervisor and have the supervisor make the determination.

Liability in the field of corrections being what it is, most jails will not accept a suspect at booking if they claim injury, visible or not. That being the case, if the suspect claims injury out on the street, call EMS. If EMS determines that no injury exists or that the person does not need to go to the emergency room for treatment they will give you a copy of their "run sheet" which will be accepted by the jail medical screening nurse or technician when the suspect is booked.

Further an officer must per policy make every attempt to locate and identify all witnesses to the incident. This is important because it is surely true that the witnesses supervisors and/or detectives get locked into a statement are not the ones who hurt us but rather those who we miss that are subsequently identified by plaintiff's counsel.

Supervisor's Responsibilities:

1. Respond to the scene
2. Ensure medical treatment is provided to any officer or citizen involved in the incident.
3. Determine if a Supervisor's Use of Force package is needed.
4. Obtain names of the suspect's treating physician and nurse.
5. Photograph all visible officer injuries and make sure injury reports are completed.
6. Photograph all suspects whether injured or not.
7. Interview the suspect on audiotape.
8. Interview all witnesses on audiotape.
9. Ascertain if any video footage is available through police dashboard cameras, business cameras or other means. If citizens have recorded the incident on cell-phone cameras attempt to obtain a copy if possible. *In the case of officer involved shootings it may be necessary for investigators to obtain search warrants to seize cell phone video evidence if they are not volunteered by the citizen.

CHAPTER 5

REPORTING USE OF FORCE

It may come as a surprise that some agencies do not require an investigation or use of force report unless a suspect is injured. Examination of their investigative paperwork would then indicate that 100% of suspects who have force used upon them are injured. This is absurd. When those incidents occur with no injury (by the way these types of incidents are the ones that, for some reason, seem to get an agency sued more frequently than larger more violent use of force encounters) no paperwork is generated. Instead of having an ample paper trail (officer's use of force and supervisor's investigative reports as well as photos and suspect, witness statements) to fend off an unmeritorious civil suit, an agency has no paperwork at all.

At the opposite end of the reporting spectrum is the agency that requires that their officers fill out a use of force report for everything, even when no force is used. As an example, some agencies require officers file or submit a report when they draw their pistols. The notion here is that they can prove later on after an incident shooting that they drew their pistols "X" number of times without firing a shot. Once again, this is absurd. Knowing cops as I do, two things are probably going to happen here, A) An officer won't draw his pistol when he should because he's too lazy to do the report, or B) An officer will draw his pistol and simply not fill out the paperwork. Regardless, it's a silly requirement.

It is absolutely true that an officer's use of force report protects him as well as the agency. Reporting is the means by which officers who have done the right thing articulate how and why they did it. Use of force by officers is an expected part of the job and the subsequent report is the justification and explanation of why it was required and how it was performed and most importantly – why it was objectively reasonable.

If a report is not completed or if an officer testifies to something during a civil trial or deposition on a use of force which was not included in the report the accusation will always be that they are lying. Put in the vernacular, "If it ain't on paper, it didn't happen."

Use of force in "enlightened" agencies has undergone a transition over several years. 20 years ago little, if any reportage was necessary. In a Jim Webb *Dragnet* kind of way it was, "Just the facts," and written in this stilted police language:

"On the above date and time the below listed officer encountered the aforementioned suspect in the described location. The suspect became verbally offensive and exhibited pre-attack body postures to the reporting officer. The reporting officer, after numerous loud, verbal commands to cease and desist, applied Oleoresin Capsicum chemical irritant spray to the suspect's facial area and visual system. Using reasonable force I employed a straight arm bar technique and was able to escort him to the ground. The suspect was taken into custody without further incident."

What the officer really meant to say was, *"I responded to a large fight call at Joe's Pub. The suspect told me to, "Fuck off," several times. The suspect dropped his right foot back into a boxer's type of stance, raised his fists and said, "Come on!" I told him he was under arrest and to put his hands behind his back. He refused. I drew my pepper spray and sprayed him in the eyes and face for three seconds from a distance of about seven feet. The suspect grabbed his eyes, screamed and bent over. I grabbed his left arm and pushed him down onto the floor. I handcuffed him behind his back. EMS was called and examined the suspect and determined he was uninjured. The suspect was transported by Wagon 88 to the Clark County Jail for disorderly conduct.*

Overall police reporting was done this way at the time not just use of force reports. Further, the opinion at the time was that you did not want to state what you actually did. Heaven forbid that you write in a report, "I punched the suspect in the face." Rather the thinking was that you made general statements in keeping with the language of use of force policies at the time, i.e. "I used hand strikes against the subject's structural areas." What was this supposed to mean? That you followed the suspect home and hit his house? Other examples are "using departmentally taught subject control techniques," or "the reporting officer struck the subject in the right common peroneal nerve (usually misspelled by the way) motor point in his thigh causing a motor dysfunction" (he knee struck him in the right thigh which resulted in a charley horse).

This was oftentimes repeated by supervisors in their investigative report on the use of force. "The suspect resisted arrest and the force used (fill in the blank) by the officer was within department policy."

The irony here is that during a proper investigation or review of an officer's use of force these "control techniques" or any general terms will be required to be described or explained. How can a proper determination be made on whether a use of force was reasonable (within the law) if proper descriptions of what the suspect said and did and what the officer said and did are not given?

Trainer George T. Williams of Cutting Edge Training has written an excellent book title, *Force Reporting for Every Cop* (Jones and Bartlett Publishers; 2005). In it George describes the importance of the use of force report and the reporting process:

> "Always remember the Outstanding Report Rule: A good report is first written, and then rewritten. An outstanding report is a good report that is edited, then rewritten, re-edited, and then rewritten some more.
>
> "Remember, the force response narrative report is probably the primary instrument that you and your agency's defense counsel will be using to defend you actions.
>
> "The following is a sad fact, but something that every police officer wearing a badge should understand: An attorney's job

is not to see the truth. Rather, an attorney's job is to seek weakness in the opposing case and win for his client. Some may attempt to label this statement "attorney bashing." It is not. It simply states the facts as the profession of law is practiced in the courts of America. Be aware that opposing counsel, during both the criminal prosecution of the suspect *and* the officer's civil defense, will comb a force response narrative report along with every piece of evidence and document related to the case for any weakness in the account of the officer's actions. They are looking to exploit the weaknesses of every officer's case."

Therefore, we must document as clearly as possible the suspect's actions and our actions before, during and after the use of force. Included in this documentation is the type and nature of the call and relevant notes from dispatch. If you've been to the location before or dealt with the suspect(s) on prior incidents including use of force or violence at the address make sure you include that. For instance, on a recent use of force that I was involved in and the subsequent application of the Taser and physical force against a 17 year old suspect diagnosed with Schizophrenia my partner and I learned from the caller that the subject had threatened suicide with a knife. When we pulled into the parking area the caller yelled to us that we had just driven past the subject on our way in. That he had arrived at her apartment drank most of a fifth of gin and poured a large number of pills down his throat before grabbing the knife and holding it to his own throat. We did not know if this subject was still armed with the knife or other weapons. As we turned our vehicle around and exited the parking lot, we called out to the juvenile to stop. He began running away from us through a local park. We caught up with him and took control with my partner firing the Taser into his back and then both of us forcing his arms behind his back once he fell to the ground.

All of the information gathered via dispatch call notes, yelled to us by the caller and developed by our senses was included in the report. Including the juvenile refusing to show his hands, holding them in front of his waist (which necessitated me drawing my service pistol and flanking out away from my partner should he still have the knife and deadly force be necessary) and then him giving the finger to my partner and refusing to get down on the ground.

After the incident we found out from his caretaker that he had been previously controlled by our agency with the Taser. Although this was not known at the time and could not be used to justify the application of the ECD, it was still entered into our report and supervisor's investigation to document the subject's mindset and proclivity for resisting. He was not arrested but was rather "Pink Slipped" or involuntarily committed – his caretaker had arranged for him to be committed at a facility as he had been living on the street abusing Cocaine and Marijuana for over a month.

The modern approach to report writing is: First person, past tense and active voice of the verb.

First person means that the report is written from the officer's perspective by using the pronoun 'I'. This is in comparison with the old style of third person writing, i.e. "This officer" or "The reporting officer..."

Past tense is used because the action occurred in the past versus present tense. An example would be, "I punched the suspect in the stomach" versus "Punching the suspect in the stomach..."

Active voice is the normal way we speak and write. Passive on the other hand has the subject receiving the action of the verb, "The suspect was punched in the stomach," or "The suspect is controlled by a joint lock." Passive voice usually includes what's called an auxiliary verb such as: is, was, are, am. Was controlled, is punched, etcetera.

Noted Federal Law Enforcement Training Center instructor John Bostain and his co-workers at FLETC in Glynco, Georgia have commented that they instruct their students to report the *facts* not *conclusions*. Examples are the phrase "he resisted arrest" or "I controlled him." These are conclusions which will be reached and documented by supervisors or internal affairs personnel who review the officer's report. It is far better for the officer to report what she did and said and the results as well as what the suspect did and said and their responses. In this way the *facts* are given and not the officer's conclusions which are oftentimes scant on details.

I believe that if two or more officers are involved in a use of force that each officer should write his or her own report. This will serve as the primary instrument for the officer(s) to: justify their use of force against the suspect in an internal investigation; convict the suspect of criminal charges such as resisting arrest in a court of law; defend their actions in a citizen complaint of excessive force and serve as memory aid, court document in any civil litigation. That requires good and *separate* documentation from all officers involved.

A note here, it is entirely possible and understandable that two officers involved in the same incident will have different, possibly conflicting reports. Although we will cover this in more detail in the chapter on the actual investigation, it is important to understand that even the best report is not the actual incident. Too many officers have been disciplined based on a supervisor's opinion that they are lying, i.e. other officers or witness statements or videos tell a different story than the officer's report.

MEMORY

Human memory is an interesting subject. To get a better understanding of how the brain works and specifically under stress I would suggest – Robert Sapolsky's excellent *Why Zebras Don't Get Ulcers* (Third Edition, Owl Books, 2004). When an officer (or for that matter any witness) has experienced an SNS (Sympathetic Nervous System – fight or flight) response their memory is substantially impacted. The *autonomic nervous system* is compared to the voluntary nervous system. From Sapolsky's book, "the voluntary nervous system is a conscious one. You decide to move a muscle and it happens. The set of nerve projections to places like sweat glands carry messages that are relatively involuntary and automatic. It is thus termed the *autonomic nervous system*, and it has everything to do with your response to stress. One half of this system is activated in response to stress, one half is suppressed." If/when an officer is involved in a dynamic event he may go from the higher functioning Parasympathetic Nervous System of his brain to the SNS. The brain literally changes the way it does business with the limbic system (amygdala, hypothalamus, hippocampus and more) or the emotional centers of the brain taking control. This is responsible for perceptual distortions such as tunnel vision, auditory exclusion, or time distortions. Short-term memory versus long-term memory and emotionally charged memory are apparently stored in the brain differently. Sapolsky states that in studies the SNS improved memory retention up to a point, "People in the learning and memory business refer to this as an "inverse-U" relationship. As you go from no stress to a moderate, transient amount of stress – the realm of stimulation – memory improves. As you then transition into severe stress, memory declines."

Thrown into the mix of the SNS response and the perceptual distortions that may occur is the issue of inattentional blindness. Brought to the law enforcement community through the fine works of Bill Lewinski, PhD and the research conducted by his Force Science Research Center, www. forcescience.org inattentional blindness is oftentimes explained by the Gorilla experiment conducted by Christopher Chabris and Daniel Simons which is detailed in their book *The Invisible Gorilla* (Broadway Paperbacks, 2009). Chabris and Simons engineered a videotaped experiment in a hallway at Harvard University. Chabris and Simons had graduate students in white t-shirts and black t-shirts moving around and passing basketballs back and forth to each other. When viewing the tape volunteers were asked to count the number of passes by the white clad participants and ignore the people in the black t-shirts. You can and should view this experiment right now at www.theinvisiblegorilla.com before you read on.

After viewing they were asked how many passes were made by the participants in white. Varying answers are given but the truth is that it doesn't matter, the sole purpose of the experiment was to see if those volunteers tested saw the person in the gorilla suit walk into the middle of the screen, stop, thump its chest and then walk off.

According to Chabris and Simons in their book, "Amazingly, roughly half of the subjects in our study did not notice the gorilla! What made the gorilla invisible? This error of perception results from a lack of attention to an unexpected object, so it goes by the scientific name "inattentional blindness."

How does all this relate to use of force investigative reports? Officers can only report what they were paying attention to and within the ability of their recall or memory. This is not to excuse all misstatements in use of force reporting. As noted police psychologist, researcher and trainer Alexis Artwohl has stated, "We define a lie as the person consciously and knowingly telling you something different than what's in their head.

They know that it is red but they tell you that it is green." (ASLET Int. Seminar, 1997)

Just remember that regardless of how good an officer's use of force report is, it is not the actual event.

Over the years we have learned that officers who are involved in a traumatic event such as a shooting are better served by waiting at least one to two sleep cycles prior to having an interview with investigating detectives. This is still true for officers involved in a serious resisting arrest incident or violent application of non-deadly force. If the officer has been involved in a real knock-down-drag-out fight it might be advisable to wait until they are up to reporting the incident properly.

Popular today is the computer template type use of force report which includes a checklist as part of the report. This type of report may have diagrams of the human body for the officer to indicate locations of force applications such as Taser probes or baton strikes and/or checkboxes for various use of force options – ☐ empty hand strikes, ☐ OC spray, ☐ knee strikes, etc... If these types of report are used it is vital that officers understand that the lists and checkboxes are there to supplement the narrative section of the report, never to replace it. If these reports are available via the Mobile Digital Termianl in the patrol vehicle less downtime occurs than if an officer has to go out of service and head to the station to complete the paperwork.

A note here on dictated reports. As an expert witness I've had to deal with officer reports which are dictated and subsequently transcribed into writing by a secretary or firm hired to do such. I don't like them. I think that they lack the first person "telling the story" view that is so important in a use of force report.

To wrap up this section on memory let me refer to research completed by Dr. Andy Morgan psychiatrist from Yale University on more than 500 soldiers completing escape and evasion training at Fort Bragg. After being interrogated (*simulated* military enemy interrogation but high stress) one in three of the participants (Special Forces personnel, some pilots and Marines) were unable to properly identify their interrogator, often even getting the gender wrong, this despite being in the room alone with the interrogator for over half an hour. Live line-ups resulted in a (26%) accuracy rate, photo spread (33%) accuracy and (49%) in a photo sequence. From the study, "These data provide robust evidence that eyewitness memory for persons encountered during events that are personally relevant, highly stressful, and realistic in nature may be subject to substantial error." (*Accuracy of eyewitness memory for persons encountered during exposure to highly intense stress*; Morgan, Hazlett, Doran, Garrett, Hoyt, Thomas, Baranoski, Southwick; International Journal of Law and Psychiatry; 27 (2004) 265-279

SUPERVISOR'S REPORTS OF INVESTIGATION

Once again written in the same: First person, past tense and active voice, the supervisor's ROI (Report of Investigation) contains what they did from their perspective as well as suspect and witness statements transcribed (★These don't have to be exact because the cassette, DVD or digital file containing the actual recorded interviews should be maintained by the agency as well as part of the case file). Since the officer's report stands on its own it is not necessary to copy the entire officer statement within the ROI however, with computer generated reports parts or the whole if necessary can be "copied and pasted" very easily.

Supervisors must ensure that use of force reports are completed by the involved officers. A supervisor's job is to make sure these reports are complete and acceptable. A supervisor does not do an officer, his agency and indeed himself any good by accepting an incomplete or poorly written report. In this day and age of computers, it is very easy for an officer to fix and improve their report versus the day of hand-written reports. As an FTO (Field Training Officer) I kept a red pen in my briefcase while reviewing my rookie's reports. If it was a crap sandwich of a report, out came the red pen and the admonishment, "Do it again and better."

It is the responsibility of the front-line supervisor to check and either accept or reject the officer's use of force report. It is the job of the shift commander to accept the supervisor's use of force package and so on up the chain-of-command. This means that each reader of the lower rung personnel's work must pay attention to the written reports to provide the clearest picture how and why the officer did the right thing. It is simply not enough for an officer to be good at the physical aspects of use of force if they cannot properly document their actions. Same too for a supervisor – they must be able to properly investigate and report.

Officers who are unable to complete a report due to injury, for instance, should still be interviewed by a supervisor and make an official statement. On one case I worked the officer's statement was never taken in the months after the incident and he was subsequently charged with criminal offenses. If the investigating supervisor had interviewed the officer (who went to the hospital that night with his injuries) he would have found the officer had a perfectly sound explanation for his actions. If the officer refuses to make a statement citing his Fifth Amendment rights, this may mean compelling the officer to make a statement under Garrity. This will be covered more in Chapter 7.

My definition of the use of force reporting process includes:

"Explaining to the best of the officer's ability, working with a supervisor the totality of the circumstances of the use of force including: time, environment, suspect(s) words and actions, officers perceptions, officer's words and actions, attempts at control/responses, restraint device application, injuries, follow-up care and transport."

It is not as simple as, "Officer Jones arrived on scene, kicked ass, left scene." This has never been true in my career and is especially not true today.

We as law enforcement officers do the right thing, post incident it is time to properly document why and how we did that.

CHAPTER 6

SUPERVISOR RESPONSE

Anytime an officer uses force she must, per agency policy, notify her supervisor. The supervisor must go to the scene and first and foremost check the physical welfare of involved officers and innocent citizens. Secondly the supervisor must check on the suspect to see what, if any, injuries they have and that EMS has been called. Supervisors must take command of the use of force investigation. In the use of non-deadly force incidents they are responsible for the total investigation including interviews, photographs, evidence (such as dashboard or other video evidence) as well as documenting their investigation with a detailed report and ultimately rendering a conclusion as to whether the use of force was appropriate.

In the case of a officer involved shooting that supervisor needs to follow proper police protocols about the preservation of the scene and evidence as well as ensure that notifications are made to the chain of command, evidence teams and may ultimately relinquish investigative control to a detective supervisor. In deadly force incidents, regardless of whether a suspect, citizen or officer was hit, a full-scale shots fired investigation should be commenced. Just because an officer did not hit anything with his gunfire does not mean that it should not be fully investigated as an officer involved shooting. Without a full-scale investigation evidence may be lost, witnesses not interviewed and the full protection to the agency and officer of a proper investigation not available. In smaller agencies, the supervisor may be one of the primary investigators per policy even in officer involved shootings. Even in cases where another agency such as the county Sheriff or State Police investigates, they cannot order the involved employee to do anything because they are outside the chain of command. The supervisor is the agency's authority figure who must order or compel the officer (employee's) cooperation.

The importance of a proper supervisor response and investigation is seemingly readily apparent in officer involved shootings (I say seemingly because I have seen several cases where investigations were not done even though supervisors and administrators should have known better and in fact had been warned of the ramifications of a failure to investigate) but is sometimes ignored.

Solid agency policy and standard operating procedures ensure that things are done properly protecting the officer involved, the agency, any other crime victims and ultimately documenting the process in a report that can withstand courtroom scrutiny as well as disciplinary system review if warranted.

🗁 CASE STUDY:

"Charlie" was a good and conscientious officer. Working an off-duty job at a department store in his city, it was closing time. He was standing inside the front door area as he had locked the entrance door already and was monitoring the cashier area as the remaining customers checked out. "Billy" was a local crack-head who by his own admission had been smoking rock Cocaine all day. Billy denied that he entered the store to rob it to further his day long binging, claiming instead to have gotten hungry and gone to the store to get something to eat. Funny, when Billy approached the cash register he didn't have any food but rather a small pack of paintbrushes (never ran into a crack Cocaine "geeker" who in mid smoking binge suddenly decided to redecorate but, be that as it may, that's his story.)

When the cashier opened the drawer to cash out the customer in front of him, Billy saw his opportunity. Aggressively thrusting himself over the counter, he pushed the 16 year old cashier out of the way and grabbed as much cash as he could. The cashier screamed out and Charlie, the off-duty officer, sprang into action. Running up behind the robbery suspect he grabbed him from behind in a "bear-hug." The two men fought throughout the checkout area and into the foyer (the area between the interior and exterior glass doors). At some point Charlie feeling that he was losing the battle, fired two rounds from his department owned semi-auto pistol. One of the rounds missed, the other hit the suspect in the right cheek. Billy only fought harder. The two men continued to struggle and smashed through the glass exit door. Charlie fired again with two rounds missing and one round smashing through Billy's right femur, shattering the upper leg bone. Billy attempted to limp away but was taken into custody by Officer Charlie in the parking lot area.

The agency's detective bureau rolled on the shooting with photos of the crime scene taken and evidence collected.

Officer Charlie was taken to the police station and without time off to gather his thoughts was ordered to make a statement. It reads in part:

> "I then went over the register grabbed the male in a headlock pulling him away from the register and Ms. Smith at which time we started to fight inside the store between the counter and the exit doors. While myself and the male were fighting in the store I was condering about the peoples in the store. I was feel that if this male was not apprehended at this point he was going to cause harmed myself and the people till inside the store. While he was fighting the male was over powering this report officer throwing me around inside the store cause me to fear for my life in the fight this Officer told him to stopped he was under arrest at which time he started to fight must harder at this time I pushed my weapon fire the one time while we were fight going through the frist set of door leading in another short hall. While we were inside the hallway the male was still fight with this Officer at which time the male was still overpowing this Officer at which time discharge my weapon again trying to apprehend him but he fought me harder. When fell through the other door which lead to the outside of the store him and I were on the ground fighting at with time he over power the officer at which time I till fear for my safety when I discharge my weapon because he was still a threat to myself and other and he was desperate, after he fell to the ground"

This officer written use of force report was accepted by his supervisor and entered into the permanent record.

The supervisor submits a question and answer confidential with his investigative report. It is clearly marked Police Department Internal Affairs Division (Garrity Rights). Most of these questions have nothing to do with the actual shooting but rather focus in on Charlie's use of agency equipment (pistol) on an off-duty job which is forbidden by agency policy. The supervisor never conducts a detailed interview of the officer and yet in his conclusion writes, "In totality of the circumstances, it is my opinion that the use of deadly force implemented by Off. Charlie cannot be justified in this case, however, upon reviewing the regulations regarding firearms in the policy/procedure manual I am hesitant to recommend charges against Officer Charlie regarding the use of his firearm in this incident."

We see the co-mingling of the internal affairs investigation on the fairly unimportant issue of carrying an agency pistol off-duty with the much more important criminal investigation involving the use of deadly force by a member of service.

To add insult to injury (no detailed interview with the officer) the local prosecutor's office indicts the officer for Felonious Assault based on large part of a videotape of the shooting in which they state that the suspect posed no threat to the officer and was running away through the parking area when he was shot.

We will refer to this case in several parts but let's focus on the supervisory response and officer statement.

Should the officer's statement have ever been accepted? In my opinion, no it should not. Would a detective or detective supervisor accept such a statement from a victim of a serious crime? Once again, I believe that professionals would not. If the officer is traumatized, has memory issues or is inarticulate in his writing, a tape recorded statement would be far better. Regardless, a professional police investigator in a police shooting should not accept just a written report and should also audio record the interview – not trusting his memory and getting a permanent record of the officer's statement including voice inflection and nuance.

I was hired by the Fraternal Order of Police to work with the defense team as an expert witness. As part of that preparation I interviewed Charlie.

First of all I asked that he tell me everything: what he saw and heard; up to and including how the suspect smelled (it is common knowledge among street officers that crack Cocaine users oftentimes have very poor hygiene and emit a foul body odor); even what he was feeling, including his fears. Even in the oral interview, there were several times that I had to ask prompting questions. After the interview I asked if anyone had talked to him like I had. He said no, no one from his agency had conducted such an interview.

Here's what I found out. Despite outweighing the suspect by over two hundred pounds, Billy had tossed Officer Charlie around, "like Hulk Hogan." At one time after pushing the officer backward into some shelving in the checkout area, Charlie who still had both hands around the suspect in a "bear-hug" felt the suspect's hand "fishing for my pistol" and actually getting his hand on the officer's semi-auto but was unable to pull it from the holster. When the two crashed into the foyer area between the outside and inside glass doors the 50 plus year old asthmatic officer who, had been seriously injured years before when he was shot by a suspect, believed he was losing the fight and became physically exhausted. It was at this time, with a suspect who had already attempted to disarm him, that he fired the first two shots. The result was a more aggressive suspect who crashes with the officer holding onto him through the glass exit door and lands on top of the officer. The suspect then stands and dives a hand into his pocket (a metal crack pipe was later recovered in his pocket). The officer begins shooting again with three shots fired one of which, shatters the leg.

We will examine the video evidence in this case later in this manual but suffice to say that this officer after more than 30 plus years in law enforcement in which he was shot by a drug suspect while working undercover for another agency, and 25 years with this agency was charged with a felony in large part due to a botched and unprofessional investigation by his own agency.

I'll cut to the chase and tell you we were able, after interviewing the officer and examining the video evidence used to indict him, to have the case successfully dismissed. Sadly his elderly Father had passed away prior to the dismissal and went to his grave without seeing his son vindicated.

This is the type of result that can occur when an ill-informed agency: develops and maintains a poor policy; fails to train its supervisors in use of force investigations; fails to train its officers in use of force and proper reporting; and fails to implement all of these things in an actual incident.

Recommendations for supervisor's use of force investigative responses:

- Respond to the scene
- Ensure injured officers, citizens and arrestees get care
- Audio record statements from the suspect(s) and witnesses
- Take photographs of officer(s) injuries
- Take photographs of suspect regardless of whether injured or not
- Take photos of the incident scene if environment factors into the incident (lighting, distance, furniture placement, cluttered crime scene, etc.)

Once again a "checklist" is an excellent idea to ensure that all the material required is obtained and included.

All of these reports should be compiled into a "package" with appropriate copies distributed.

Most important of the supervisor duties is to; establish totality of the circumstances by investigating the facts of the case through the evidence and interviews and then render a conclusion or "opinion." This conclusion is whether the supervisor believes the force used was objectively reasonable based on the totality of the circumstances considering the officer's reasonable perceptions. This cannot be a "rush to judgment" but a well thought out determination based on all the facts, policy and the law.

COMMON TRAPS & MISTAKES: THE TACTICAL CRITIQUE

The trap of supervisors falling into a "tactical critique" rather than a proper use of force investigation is a concept that California law enforcement trainer and writer Jeff Cope first mentioned in a series of columns on LawOfficer.com.

I'll give a hypothetical example:

Deputy Smithers has stopped a motorist on the local section of the State highway which runs through his jurisdiction. It is 11:00 pm, the motorist has been weaving and so the Deputy suspects the driver is drunk. Without calling in the vehicle stop to dispatch per policy, Smithers walks up to the stopped four-door and sees the male driver has an open container of liquor held between his legs and reeks of the odor of alcoholic beverage. Dep. Smithers shines his flashlight into the passenger compartment and identifies himself, "Dep. Smithers of the Woodson County Sheriff's Office sir. May I see your driver's license and proof of insurance?" Smithers watches as the red and bleary eyed driver turns his head and looks up at him without speaking or moving. Dep. Smithers making the decision to place the suspect under arrest for OVI, reaches into the passenger compartment through the open window to secure the bottle of liquor as evidence and a possible weapon. The suspect suddenly comes to life and clamps down both hands on the Deputy's arm. The suspect, who has never placed the vehicle into Park or turned off the ignition stomps on the accelerator pulling Smithers along. As the vehicle gains speed, Smithers fearing that his is going to be dragged to death or fall under the wheels of the car, draws his duty pistol and fires five quick shots toward the driver. One bullet enters the rear of his neck severing his upper spinal column and turning him into a quadriplegic. Deputy Smithers falls to the roadway breaking his arm and sustaining a concussion, as the vehicle careens out of control off the road and strikes a tree.

Even though the local prosecutor has determined that the shooting was within the law, in the use of force investigation the supervisor focuses in on the Deputy's policy violations – not calling in the vehicle stop as well as the tactical mistakes he made: not waiting for back-up and reaching into the passenger compartment instead of first removing the driver. Because he went to the Emergency Room that night for his injuries and was never interviewed, the supervisor's conclusion is based solely on the original comments Smithers made in the ER. There was no follow-up interview. A dashboard camera tape depicts the events as they unfold but contains no audio. The supervisor states in his report that Dep. Smithers created the jeopardy by not following agency policy and training as well as standard police tactics.

Deputy Smithers' shooting is found to be excessive force by his agency and he is fired. Sadly, the deputy is terminated without the agency consulting its own use of force instructor or training bureau. The local news media gets a copy of the supervisor's report and dashboard tape based on a public records request. The agency's name is drug through the mud and the Deputy is portrayed by the talking heads as an incompetent thug.

Subsequently in the arbitration hearing the union brings in an outside expert who calls the agency to task for their outdated policy and the conclusion of the supervisor's investigation.

Result? The arbitrator rules against the county and the Deputy is returned to full duty with back pay. A resulting civil suit against the agency pits the management of the agency against its deputies and training staff. All because the agency conducted a tactical debrief instead of a proper use of deadly force investigation.

Perhaps you think this hypothetical situation is extreme and out of the realm of possibility? Sadly a simple Google® search on police use of force will provide a large number of examples of this very type of process taking place.

The Supreme Court in the Graham case stated, "reasonableness of a particular use of force must be judged from the perspective of a reasonable officer on the scene, rather than with the 20/20 vision of hindsight." Also, "The calculus of reasonableness must embody allowance for the fact that police officers are often forced to make split-second judgments – in circumstances that are tense, uncertain, and rapidly evolving – about the amount of force that is necessary in a particular situation."

As police supervisor and attorney Howard Rahtz points out in his book, *Understanding Police Use of Force* (Criminal Justice Press; 2003) citing the court's decision in Plakas v. Drinski (7th Circuit, 1994) "We do not return to the prior segments of the event and, in light of hindsight, reconsider whether the prior police decisions were correct." Rahtz states in his book, "The rulings in these three cases (Plakas, Scott v. Henrich and Schultz v. Long) affirmed the principle that deadly-force incidents must be judged from the precise moment the "seizure," i.e. deadly force, occurs."

> "We must never allow the theoretical, sanitized world of our imagination to replace the dangerous and complex world that policeman face every day. What constitutes 'reasonable' action

may seem quite different to someone facing a possible assailant that to someone analyzing the question at leisure."

United States v. Sanchez (9ᵗʰ Circuit; 1990)

"Detached reflection cannot be demanded in the presence of an uplifted knife."

Brown v. United States, 256 U.S. 961, at 963 (1921)

It is entirely possible that the officer could have made tactical blunders and mistakes which may have created the jeopardy but since the use of force is to be judged at the "moment the trigger is pulled" or force is used, it is irrelevant. The question is at the moment of the application of force based on reasonable perceptions and the totality of the circumstances whether the force used was objectively reasonable. In the vast majority of situations, officers don't shoot people for drunk driving, open container, speeding or whatever the original nature of the call or stop. Officers shoot people because they believe that at the moment they pulled the trigger that their life or the life of another was in danger of death or serious bodily harm. The question up to the investigator is whether those acts are reasonable?

Now, there are cases specifically examining the use of the Taser which question whether the use of force was objectively reasonable based on the foreseeable outcome of the application of the ECD (Electronic Control Device) to control a subject. As an example, in New York City officers were confronted with a naked EDP (Emotionally Disturbed Person) atop a security door swinging a long florescent light bulb. A police lieutenant ordered that an officer fire the Taser at the subject prior to air bags being deployed. The result was the fall and subsequent death of the subject. Even more tragic was the ultimate suicide of the police lieutenant after being investigated for excessive use of force. Taser International and its programs have always cautioned against using the ECD on subjects who, after being incapacitated and falling, are at risk of death or serious bodily harm.

The 9ᵗʰ Circuit Court of Appeals decision in Bryan v. McPherson concluded that Officer McPherson's use of the Taser was excessive (although they subsequently awarded him immunity because they stated the law at the time of the incident was not clearly established). In this case the 9ᵗʰ Circuit cited Graham, "whether the officers' actions are 'objectively reasonable' in light of the facts and circumstances confronting them." However the court further examined whether Officer MePherson did not consider "less intrusive means" in their decision. Jack Ryan, JD writes in "The Law and Best Practices of Successful Police Operations (Public Agency Training Council; 2010), "It should be noted that this **"less intrusive means"** language has never been an element of use of force analysis by the United States Supreme Court and is contrary to all of the other United States Circuits." For officer and agencies within the 9th Circuit, Jack Ryan's "Bottom Line" points on the Taser as listed in his book are:

- TASER and other electronic control devices are intermediate weapons thus policies which place TASER at a lower level must be changed.
- Use (at least in the probe mode as here) requires a strong government interest which this opinion indicates is "an immediate threat" by the subject to the officer.
- Warning is important and should be done unless exigent circumstances exist.

★The 9th Circuit has expressed concerns of the use of pepper spray as well. In *Headwaters Forest Def. v. County of Humboldt*, 276 F.3d 1125 (9th Cir. 2002), "they held that a jury could conclude that pepper spray was more than a "minimal intrusion: as it caused "intense pain..., an involuntary closing of the eyes, a gagging reflex, and temporary paralysis of the larynx."

The 9th Circuit Court states in *McPherson*, "The "most important" factor under *Graham* is whether the suspect posed an "immediate threat to the safety of the officers or others." Their decision states, "A desire to resolve quickly a potentially dangerous situation is not the type of governmental interest that, standing alone, justifies the use of force that many cause serious injury," and "the objective facts must indicate that the suspect poses an immediate threat to the officer or a member of the public."

Much of this second-guessing is based on the *"split-second decision making syndrome"* as developed and promulgated by the late James Fyfe. Fyfe and this concept are supported by a few criminal justice professors or commentators such as William Geller and Michael Scott.

From the Police Executive Research Forum book *Deadly Force: What We Know* cited earlier, we read:

> "Thus, officers were asked to think about the shooting decision not only as an instantaneous "Should I pull the trigger?" question, but as part of a series of decisions spanning space and time. These decisions would encompass such issues as: "Should I engage this suspect? Should I engage him *alone*? Should I engage him *now*? What is the best way to enter the scene? What do I need to know about the suspect, the scene, any possible third parties who might be present, and so forth to improve my chances of controlling this encounter and having it come out in a proper fashion? These and other such questions discussed at length elsewhere in this volume were addressed."

> "By "backing up" in time from the "split-second" decision to pull or not pull the trigger, some researchers have charted a course for a new body of research on "averted shootings." Averted shootings are situation with potential to escalate into use of deadly force by police but that, through officer skill or other circumstances, are resolved without the officer(s) firing a weapon. Much of the best tactical training literature for many years has focused on how officers, through proper approaches to and handling of suspects, can apprehend potentially dangerous persons with minimal risk."

This is not to say that the tactics and techniques that officers use approaching as well as dealing with suspects, stops, searches and responses is not a vital part of police work. Training *must* cover these issues and front-line supervisors *must* ensure that their officers are engaging in safe and sound tactics and responses. That said, we must not judge an officer's use of force based on these tactics and responses.

Fyfe was extreme in his views believing (according to Geller and Scott) that he "urged police departments to reconsider completely the routine of arming of off-duty police suggested more than a decade ago (1980) that further research may well demonstrate that both officers and the community will be safer if we "require off-duty police to leave their guns in their lockers with the rest of their uniforms."

> "Fyfe's data showed, for example, that off-duty officers who remained passive during tavern robberies survived unhurt, while many officers who tried to intervene were wounded and killed."

One thing is for certain; if an officer never showed up for work that day, did nothing on patrol or did not respond to dangerous calls shootings by police would be virtually nonexistent. I wonder if this is what some of these "theorists and academics" want?

Modern officer survival training encourages off-duty officers to not get involved in incidents if at all possible and to be the best witness that they can. However if they are randomly targeted or are specifically the target of a revenge type of deadly assault, an officer's life is a heck of a price to pay for such a nonsensical notion.

Geller and Scott refer to officers who paint themselves and the suspects into a corner via their tactics where the suspect's only reasonable action is aggression, a deadly threat or action and the officer's only response is with gunfire. The suspect always has the option to surrender peacefully and to not resort to violent assault against the law enforcement officer. An officer when faced with a suspect armed with a gun (depending on time, distance and availability of cover) cannot afford to wait to "read the suspect's intent" as so many academicians have suggested. Does this sometimes mean that an innocent homeowner or concealed carry permit holder may be shot? Yes. Tragedies do occur like this when a subject, for whatever reasons, points a toy gun at a police officer.

Geller and Scott again quote Fyfe:

> "Improper shootings (or improper uses of nonlethal force) by police can helpfully be classified in two basic categories: "willful and wrongful use of force by officers" (brutality) and

"police violence emanating from simple incompetence" (Fyfe 1989c: 465, 467), which it is suggested, may be called simply "unnecessary force."

All of this is of course ignores the 7th Circuit's decision in Plakas v. Drinski:

> "Other than random attacks, all such cases begin with the decision of a police officer to do something, to help, to arrest, to inquire. If the officer had decided to do nothing then no force would have been used. In this sense the police always causes the trouble. But it is trouble which the police officer is sworn to cause, which society pays him to cause and which, if kept within constitutional limits, society praises the officer for causing."

It is a use of force investigative blunder to focus in on officer tactics prior to the use of force other than to develop and document *totality of the circumstances*. If an officer exposes himself to risk or utilizes poor tactics he should be given a "Dutch Uncle" talk by a supervisor at the very least and sometimes disciplined, if appropriate. To include these tactical examinations with a use of force investigation is wrong and can taint or improperly influence the investigative outcome.

It is my opinion that the late James Fyfe thoughts on "the split-second decision syndrome" are false and not in keeping with the Supreme Court's decision in *Graham*, "With respect to a claim of excessive force, the same standard of reasonableness at the moment applies." "The reasonableness of a particular use of force must be judged from the perspective of a reasonable officer on the scene, rather than the 20/20 vision of hindsight."

What number of incidents in which officers *could* have used deadly force but chose not to? Unfortunately officers are oftentimes given awards for actions in incidents in which they should have used deadly force or unnecessarily exposed themselves and other officers to risk. A friend of mine who is a supervisor refers these types of incidents in which officer are praised for "restraint" as "outcome based investigations or critiques." In other words because the end result or outcome turned out well, we praise the officer.

For instance, trainer Pat Martin gave an excellent seminar titled *Shut Up and Shoot!* at the 2006 ASLET conference (American Society of Law Enforcement Trainers, an organization now sadly, no longer in existence). Mr. Martin pointed out that if you removed the 18% of officers who were ambushed by assailants when examining the 594 officers killed in the line of duty from 1995 to 2004 nearly one third of the officers killed did not use or attempt to use their own weapon. The emphasis of Mr. Martin's seminar was that over verbalizing is a form of indecision or hesitancy to shoot. By talking too much or giving too many warnings to "Drop the gun!" to an armed suspect you are thinking about talking versus shooting and you enable the suspect to act (shoot) before you can respond (fire).

Once again theorists and academicians who have never spent a day in uniform would suggest that such indecision or delay is somehow good. That we should wait to ascertain the *intent* of the suspect. In the real world of policing such delay as Pat Martin has pointed out can lead to a *tragic outcome for the officer or others.*

COMMON TRAPS & MISTAKES: SUBJECTIVE VERSUS OBJECTIVE

Hypothetical scenario:

At 1 a.m. in Gotham City, Officer Jones of the Gotham P.D. attempted to stop a vehicle that showed up on agency's "hot-sheet" as being recently stolen. As soon as Jones initiated his patrol unit's overhead lights the suspect slowed but then began a slow speed (no faster than 35 mph) pursuit through quiet residential streets. After about five minutes of calling the chase out, sufficient numbers of Gotham P.D. officers were in the area. The suspect pulled to the curb and bailed out of the sedan he was driving and ran away through backyards in the area. Several officers initiated foot pursuit including Jones, who tackled the suspect and handcuffed him in a citizen's backyard.

The suspect was brought back to the street and placed chest down against the front hood of a Gotham PD patrol vehicle which had a dashboard camera recording. The suspect began pushing his upper body off the hood of the car requiring that he be pushed down several times. The suspect pushed off the hood of the cruiser once again, thrashed his body in an attempt to get Jones to let go, turned and spit directly into Officer Jones face and eyes. Officer Jones is seen on the tape taking one step back, is heard on the audio tape stating "Fucking idiot," and striking out with his right hand punching the suspect once in the face. Jones struggles with the suspect and is able to, with the help of additional officers, force the suspect to the ground where he increases his resistance and is subsequently Tasered.

Based on a viewing of the tape, Officer Jones is charged by his supervisor with excessive use of force. The investigating supervisor stated, "It is clear by his comment after being spit on that Officer Jones was angry. I believe that his punching of the suspect was excessive force because he reacted in anger. Furthermore his actions (punching the suspect) resulted in more force being applied not less. Because of his acting in anger and the punch not controlling the suspect but rather increased the violence, it is my opinion that Officer Jones used excessive force."

It is entirely possible that Officer Jones was angry. One could argue that being assaulted by having a suspect spit directly in your face would reasonably initiate an emotional response. But the question is not whether Jones was angry. The question is whether the force used (punch to the face) was reasonable based on the totality of the circumstances. Officer Jones was already dealing with a resistive subject who, failed to stop for the lights & siren of his patrol unit; continued to attempt to evade for several minutes; attempted escape by running away; had force used against him (tackle) to apprehend him; pushed off the hood of the cruiser several times even after being handcuffed behind his back; and then spit in a police officer's face. Because Officer Jones' motive for striking the suspect, as well as his emotions (anger), are subjective in nature they are irrelevant. The question is whether a punch to the face is within the "range of reasonableness" of a reasonable officer on scene. Further, when the supervisor comments that the punch initiated further resistance and violence from the suspect, he is engaging in 20/20 hindsight. It was entirely possible that the suspect could have just as easily stopped resisting when he was struck.

In this case, regardless that the use of force caught on tape "doesn't look good," it is objectively reasonable based on the totality of the circumstances.

CHAPTER 7

THE INVESTIGATION

A couple of determinations need to be made at the onset of each use of force investigation according to such police legal authorities as attorneys Michael Brave and Randy Means. First up, is the *lawful authority to take action*. Is the officer on-duty within his jurisdiction or authorized by law to take action? This includes off-duty incidents where the officer invokes his powers or makes the statement, "I am a police officer," or "You're under arrest."

Secondly officers must have a "lawful objective." Lawful objectives include detention, arrest or involuntary mental commitment and others.

If an officer does not have lawful authority or a lawful objective in taking action, regardless of how little force is used it will be unconstitutional (outside the parameters of the law).

📁 CASE STUDY:

Officer Jones patrolled a high-crime area known for open air drug markets, assault, robberies, burglaries, prostitution and other street crimes. While on street patrol on Talbot Ave. he sees a subject walking down the sidewalk he does not know. He pulls his patrol unit to the curb, exits and approaches the male who is walking toward him. Officer Jones says to the male, "How you doing man? Can I talk to you for a minute?" The male who is now walking past the officer turns his head and says, "Nope" and continues walking away. Off. Jones then says, "I need to talk to you man," walks up to the rear of the suspect grabs his arm and the nape of his neck and forces him down to the ground on the grass of a front yard of Talbot. Officer Jones handcuffs the subject who is uninjured in the use of force. A subsequent search of the suspect finds no contraband and a check for warrants is negative. The subject is arrested for "Obstruction of Official Business" given a summons and released. The subject complains and demands to see a police supervisor.

Upon investigation we would find that the officer had neither "reasonable suspicion" nor "probable cause" to make a seizure of the subject. In Terry v. Ohio the Supreme Court allowed a brief detention by the officer when he or she has "reasonable articulable suspicion," to believe that:

1. A crime has been committed,
2. A crime is being committed, or
3. A crime is about to be committed; AND
4. The person about to be stopped is the person who did one of the above.

Although headlong flight (running away from police) might be enough in this environment to rise to the level of "reasonable suspicion" based on Illinois v. Wardlow, (Supreme Court, 2000), walking along on the sidewalk is not enough to justify a use of force to accomplish a "Terry Stop."

What we have in our hypothetical scenario is an "encounter" with no basis for a seizure. In these circumstances officers can ask to talk to the subject, ask for their I.D. or ask for an explanation but cannot force them to stop, demand their I.D. or use force against them. (LAAW Int., 2004)

★Note – officers occasionally get in trouble when they get into altercations or fights off-duty and when losing or having lost the physical fight, attempt to arrest the other party. As an example an off-duty officer who has been at a bar drinking heavily gets in a heated argument with another patron. The two agree to "take it outside." Once the fist fight starts and our officer is losing at fisticuffs he tells the other combatant, "I'm a cop and you're under arrest!" attempting to justify his actions "under color of law." Clearly such actions would be deemed not to have occurred while on-duty and the legal ramifications of an illegal "seizure" would arise.

To reiterate, whether on or off-duty the core transaction or basic reason for the stop or "seizure" must be lawful.

GOALS & PROCEDURES OF
THE USE OF FORCE INVESTIGATION

As eminent police psychologist and fellow ILEETA member Dr. Alexis Artwohl, Phd. has stated, "the goal of use of force investigations is: 1) Maximize the thoroughness and accuracy of the investigation while; 2) Minimizing the trauma to the officer and their families. Dr. Artwohl expounds that the investigator is not getting a statement about what really happened but is rather getting a statement of witness "perceptions." Determining the reality of the case or the facts of the case is based on physical evidence and these witness statements. Witnesses interviewed can be participants – the officer(s) and suspect(s) as well as observers. Their perception-based statements are based on what they: saw, heard, felt, smelled, their beliefs, attitudes, biases and expectations. Of course the more you able to learn about the person the better your ability to ascertain their influence on the person's statements. "The person may be telling the truth and they may be lying. We define a lie as they are deliberately and consciously telling you something that is different than what is in their head." Dr. Artwohl states that oftentimes police officers are disciplined based on an investigators "interpretation of their intent."

Dr. Alexis Artwohl, ASLET Seminar, Buffalo, NY, 1997

Based on perceptual narrowing that accompanies a fight or flight (Sympathetic Nervous System) response and the phenomenon of inattenttional blindness both of which we have already covered, it is entirely possible that misstatements of perceived reality can happen. (For further reading I would suggest Dr. Artwohl and Loren Christensen's book *Deadly Force Encounters* (Paladin Press, 1997).

Another fall-out of the SNS (Sympathetic Nervous System) or "fight or flight response" is how it impacts performance under stress. Why does a big, strong officer well-versed in his suspect control skills grab and pull an offender to his center and "power him or wrestle him" to the ground versus employing a more sophisticated technique? Why does an officer who is a very accomplished marksman on the range fire an entire magazine at an offender and not hit him once in an actual street encounter?

Seldom does an officer "rise to the occasion" in a serious use of non-deadly force encounter. It is even more rare in an officer involved shooting. They may perform as they have trained, but based on their reduced cognitive abilities as well as skill degradation under stress will oftentimes be unable to engage in sophisticated thinking and movement. As an example of what this may look like, take a look at how shooting and thinking deteriorates just under the stress of agency firearms qualification. Take a moment and think how you act under that small amount of stress. Do your hands shake? Do you get tunnel vision, focusing just on the target directly in front? Fumble an otherwise simple pistol reload? Were you so focused on your shooting you didn't hear the range commands?

The facts are that decision making under stress slows overall response time (reaction time plus movement time). The other part of the SNS response (fight or flight) not often talked about is "freezing" known scientifically as "hyper-vigilance." Officers overwhelmed with life threatening stimuli can lock down and do nothing (sensory overload). Ever have another motorist pull in front of the car you're driving? All you could do and did was slam on the brakes. Sophisticated movements like pumping the brakes didn't happen. The wrists, elbows and shoulders locked down on the steering wheel as your foot tried to put the brake pedal through the floor. This is why ABS (Anti-Lock Braking Systems) brakes on vehicles work. The computer within the system automatically pulses the brakes so they don't lock up, traction is increased and you have the ability to steer during the process.

The human equivalent of ABS is training. The more realistic the training program the more control of the SNS response an officer *may* have. Of course even the best officers can be blindsided, caught off guard, sucker punched, ambushed or otherwise attacked by an unseen or unknown opponent. Officers are taught and encouraged to maintain mental awareness and constantly survey their environment for threats but experience (and non-activity) has a way of lulling even the best officer into a false sense of security or non-awareness.

As Bruce Siddle from Human Factors Research has pointed out (PPCT Violent Passenger Management Training, 2001), a SNS response may be triggered by:

- Objective "threat" perceptions
- Objective "fear" perceptions
- ATP depletion (exhaustion)
- Deadly Force Startle Response

Objective Threat Perceptions Include:

- The threat is within close proximity
- The time needed to control the threat is minimal
- The officer is not confident in his/her abilities
- The threat is a new experience

Objective Fear Perceptions Include:

- Fear of death
- Fear of injury
- Fear of killing
- Fear of making an incorrect decision
- Fear of failure
- Fear of fear

Physical Exhaustion:

ATP/PC (Adenosine triphosphate / Creatine phosphate) is the first energy system the body uses but only lasts around 10 to 15 seconds. Once the ATP/PC system is exhausted, performance drops 45% within 30 seconds. Next up is the Lactic Acid System which is active from 10 seconds to two minutes. The final energy system is the Aerobic System which is dependent on conditioning.

When I was first exposed to this science it explained why I had felt a sudden drop in energy levels about 10 to 15 seconds into a use of force or resisting arrest encounter. It also explained why I experienced a corresponding drop in performance (45% according to the research). Most use of force incidents are anaerobic affairs lasting less than two minutes. They are more like a sprint than a marathon with officers dropping in performance 70% within 90 seconds.

Exhausted officers are more likely to escalate their application of force.

Deadly Force Startle Response:

- Threat is spontaneous
- Threat is unexpected
- Threat is within close proximity
- Unexpected loud noise (such as gunfire)
- Unexpected impact or touch (such as a sucker-punch)

SYMPATHETIC NERVOUS SYSTEM RESPONSES:

We know that the SNS response changes the way officers think, move, see, hear and remember. In an instant their heart rate and blood pressure increase, the SNS changes the blood flow in the body, wicking away the blood from the extremities, fueling the major organs for fight or flight. The body dumps powerful chemicals (epinephrine, norepinephrine, Glucocorticoids, glucagon, endorphins and enkephalins) into the system for pain tolerance and continued energy output. Col. Dave Grossman author of *On Combat* (PPCT Research Publications, 2004) talks about, "…then suddenly someone tries to kill you. Your body's response is total SNS arousal. PNS (Parasympathetic Nervous System) processes like digestion shut down: We don't need no stinking digestion. You guys blow the ballast and get down to the legs where I need you," in referring to incidents of soldiers and lawman in high-stress situations who void their bladders and bowels during combat.

The SNS response does a lot to explain why officers get stuck in "performance loops" wherein they repeat the same, often ineffective, technique over and over. Officers may keep knee striking, pressing the trigger of the Taser over and over or, baton striking a suspect even though he is not stopping or dropping. Higher cognitive processing is required to strike and then "stop and assess" before proceeding. This is one of the flaws of the outdated method of the "double-tap" when shooting. The thought was that officers should fire two rounds, stop and assess before continuing to shoot, possibly even transitioning to the head for follow-up shots. What we find now is that this performance under stress is virtually unheard of with most officers shooting after they perceive a deadly threat and then continuing to shoot until they perceive there is no longer a threat (the suspect is down, dropped his gun, etc.). During this period of response time to start and response time to stop a fairly large number of shots can be fired. Dr. Bill Lewinski has done significant research with his Force Science Institute in this area.

Although we hope and pray for high performance based on realistic and relevant training we understand that suboptimal physical performance as well as poor decision making can occur under a Sympathetic Nervous System response.

The investigator must factor in this knowledge of the human animal in times of peril. It does not excuse all incidents of excessive use of force but it does explain the perceptual distortions, impaired memories and inability to think and perform well.

Putting yourself in the place of the officer in that time of peril, was their use of force within the range of objective reasonableness? That's the question and the focus of the use of force investigation.

THE INTERVIEWING PROCESS

I have suggested that interviewing witnesses and suspects is an important part of the investigation, and it is. That said the question arises should the suspect be given his Miranda Rights prior to being interviewed? After all, the suspect will undoubtedly make incriminating remarks during his statement and these can potentially be used against him. Here I must advise you to consult your police legal advisor (prosecutor or private counsel) and obtain a written legal opinion.

That said, I can tell you it is the opinion of attorneys that I have consulted with that it does not violate the suspect's rights to conduct the supervisor interview without giving them Miranda. Furthermore, there have been frequent instances of these statements being used in court against suspects. The reason I am told, is because during the investigative interview the suspect is questioned as to whether they are a potential victim of an excessive use of police force. In other words, the primary goal of the interview is to ascertain if the law/civil rights of the suspect(s) has been violated. I have been told that despite these interviews possibly incriminating their clients, attorneys will oftentimes play the tape during trial because it contains material they believe is germane to the defense case.

Even if your local police legal advisor recommends you give Miranda prior to interviewing the suspect about the use of force, as in criminal investigations, most times suspects will still give statements.

During research for this book I asked police supervisors who I respect about this interview process. One supervisor pointed out that many supervisors are unable to get a good statement from the suspect because they open up the transport van door and ask, "What happened?", which frequently results in a poor direction of the interview and little comment by the suspect. Directing the interview, even if the suspect claims the officers beat him without provocation, into the use of force aspect of the encounter can elicit valuable statements.

For instance, if a suspect states that, "The officers beat the hell out of me!" He may later state that he was, "Just trying to pull away from the officers," which will totally validate the police officer's version of the events. Or a case of, "That officer didn't have to punch me in the face," can lead to further comments that he shoved the officer in order to escape or similar.

Many suspects will state in the interview that they are uninjured which may limit civil litigation claims later until they've talked to their attorney and have seen a "friendly" doctor arranged by their lawyer and then they may claim all matter of injury.

Even the most diehard anti-police witness can corroborate an officer's statement. For instance an observer who categorically states that the police didn't have to "beat that man down like that," oftentimes will confirm that the officer gave the suspect multiple verbal orders to stop and that the suspect was violently resisting. It could just be that they don't think police officers should be allowed to punch or strike a suspect.

COMMON TRAPS & MISTAKES: TOOLS

📂 CASE STUDY:

Sgt. Jim is a patrol sergeant working the nightshift. A fight breaks out at the local saloon. A follow-up call from the bar owner reports that the main combatants, a male and female, when forced to leave the bar had thrown a brick through the front window and then ran down the adjacent alley. Sgt. Jim is the first unit on scene and drives down the alleyway. As Sgt. Jim drives down the alley, he sees a male subject running in the poorly lit area to his right. All of a sudden the suspect is gone and Sgt. Jim stops his car wondering, "Did I hit him? I didn't hear or feel an impact?" He exits his patrol car and finds the suspect lying on the ground to his right. As he walks over and bends down with his flashlight to check the suspect, the female on the left side of the alley runs across the road and grabs Sgt. Jim around the belt line from behind with her hands directly on the sergeant's duty pistol. His back-up officer is now pulling directly behind him and the action is caught on his (the back-up officer's) patrol camera.

Sgt. Jim says something to the tune of, "What the hell?" and turns to his right toward the woman on his belt and swings his small (7 ½ inch) aluminum flashlight towards her. He swings three times but connects twice with the top of her head. She releases his belt and sits down on the ground. Subsequently she is treated for a laceration on the top of her skull which requires several stitches to close.

A supervisor from the local sheriff's office is brought in to investigate the use of force. Using the agency policy as his evaluation tool (which is seriously outdated and contains none of the legal parameters on the use of non-deadly force) he fails to include any of the totality of the circumstances within his examination. Relying mostly on the video (the notion that the use of force didn't look "good" and that it was readily apparent by watching the video it was excessive). Sgt. Jim's agency forbids the use of flashlights as impact weapons. Further because Sgt. Jim does not handcuff the female suspect after she is controlled the investigator comes to the conclusion that the force used was not necessary, was vindictive in nature and the sergeant never really thought the female was a threat.

All of the foregoing leads the investigator (who has no prior training in use of force investigations) to conclude based on his investigation that the force used was excessive. Sgt. Jim is fired for his excessive use of force, the investigator citing the injury caused to the female subject's head as "serious physical harm" determined it was excessive force and criminally charged Sgt. Jim with Felonious Assault. He is indicted and goes to trial. I was hired as the defense team expert by Sgt. Jim's union.

First off, I testified to the facts of the case, issues with his agency policy and police use of force at the civil service hearing on his termination. Introducing the objective reasonableness standard of the Fourth Amendment to the city manager, I also pointed out that although flashlights can be restricted by policy from being used as weapons (indeed they have a higher propensity of injury than even metal batons) "weapons of convenience" such as a flashlight in-hand can be used. This is especially true when spontaneous assaults happen such as this case. Further, the female grabbing the sergeant's duty belt, specifically his pistol, is a serious issue. Although the agency's policy mentioned flashlights and impact weapons, no in-service training had been given on empty-hand control, impact weapons or use of force. It is simply not enough to have a policy. An agency must train their officers with the policy in mind.

Another issue was the injury to the female's head. This oftentimes occurs when serious injuries such as orbits of suspect's eyes are broken by impact with the ground, or arms broken when taking a suspect to the ground. Since force is to be judged "at the moment" per the Graham decision, we cannot base our decision of reasonableness on injuries. Officers do not use force on safe padded mats on the street. Rather, force is used in cluttered, broken glass covered concrete and furniture filled living rooms. Many times officers are injured by kneeling on a rock or piece of glass or striking a secondary object when attempting to control suspects. So too are suspects injured in these environments and conditions, but the injury caused is not the question, the force used is the question.

We were successful in keeping the sergeant's job. Training in use of force for the agency's officers and supervisors would have eliminated this case.

It was interesting that when the city manager was properly educated about police use of force, he changed his opinion of the incident and began supporting the sergeant. Next up was the criminal trial.

The prosecutor brought in a supervisor who was an attorney from a large agency in my state. The prosecution's expert arrived at the conclusion that the force used was excessive and amounted to excessive force. I testified on the issue of policy not binding the sergeant like the law. Graham v. Connor standards on the use of non-deadly force (this was the case where the prosecutor asked me to read the Graham "at the moment" standard from the court's decision. I also testified on the sergeant's perceptual distortions which took place, such as his tunnel vision. The supposition of the investigator that Sgt. Jim never really felt she was a threat or he would have handcuffed her indicated severe use of 20/20 hindsight and easily disproven.

The sergeant was acquitted of the Felonious Assault. At a picnic to celebrate his acquittal my wife and I talked to Sgt. Jim's mother. She said her son was a good man. He started riding as an observer with his local P.D. when he was just 16 years old. He became a dispatcher for that agency at 18 years old, was sworn in as an officer at age 21. It broke her heart to see such a good man and police officer led across the street in handcuffs. All this grief and heartache based on an agency, investigator and prosecutor who didn't know police use of force law and use of force investigations.

COMMON TRAPS & MISTAKES: GARRITY RIGHTS

Garrity v. New Jersey, was a 1966 Supreme Court case on ticket fixing by police officers. During the agency investigation officers were ordered to answer questions and were told that if they refused they would be fired. The officers answered and were subsequently charged and convicted in criminal court. The Supreme Court ruled that the use of these statements in criminal proceedings against the officers violated their Fifth Amendment rights against self-incrimination. According to Will Aitchison's excellent book, *The Rights of Law Enforcement Officers, 5th Edition* (LRIS Publications, 2004), "As the Supreme Court later described, "the Fifth Amendment not only protects the individual against being involuntarily called as a witness against himself in a criminal prosecution but also privileges him not to answer official questions put to him in any other proceeding, civil or criminal, formal or informal, where the answers might incriminate him in future criminal proceedings." According to Aitchison in the 1967 SCOTUS case of Gardner v. Broderick, a police officer was fired after he refused to sign a waiver of immunity in an internal affairs investigation of bribery and corruption.

"The court reversed the officer's discharge, holding that the officer was discharged solely to waive a constitutional right. In language which has since become a guidepost for disciplinary investigations of law enforcement officers, the Court ruled that while a law enforcement agency can conduct an administrative investigation of an officer, it cannot in the course of that investigation compel the officer to waive his immunity necessary under *Garrity*.

Gardner thus created two separate rules. First, if an employee lawfully invokes the self-incrimination privilege under the Fifth Amendment, the employee may not be disciplined for doing so without a grant of immunity from the use of the answers in a subsequent criminal proceeding. Second, there exist affirmative limitations on an employer's ability to require answers to questions asked during an investigation of an employee – in the words of *Gardner*, the questions must be "specifically, narrowly, and directly" tailored to the employee's job."

As it has been interpreted over the years, *Garrity* requires that before a law enforcement agency questioning one of its officers can discipline the officer for refusing to answer questions, the agency must:

- Order the officer to answer the questions under threat of disciplinary actions
- Ask questions which are specifically, directly and narrowly related to the officer's duties or the officer's fitness for duty, and
- Advise the officer that the answers to the questions will not be used against the officer in criminal proceedings

Will Aitchison (2004)

I am aware of a case involving several sheriffs' office personnel and an in-custody death. The deputies were sequestered and ordered to write detailed use of force reports and submit to Internal Affairs interviews. They were told that they could not go home until the reports were completed. The union representative insured that each statement was compelled via Garrity. Even then, the reports and the inconsistencies between the statements by several deputies were used against them (*See Chapter 5) and they were charged with felonies. From manslaughter to felonious assault against the deceased prisoner (a very large, naked, violent mental patient experiencing Excited Delirium covered with his own blood, urine and feces).

During the suppression hearing the state investigator testified under oath that these use of force reports were just standard sheriff's office paperwork and as such were not protected from the Garrity requirement. A union representative outlined the totality of the circumstances (Garrity – supervisor ordering them to complete the reports and not allowing them to leave). The court ruled the statements were compelled, Garrity applied and the statements could not be used against them at trial.

Aitchison writes, "An 'order' to answer questions can be written or oral. In some cases, the order or the 'compulsion' to make a statement may even be implied. Most courts follow a two-part test, often referred to as the objective/subjective test, to determine if an employee's statements were voluntary or compelled. An employee is considered "ordered" or, in the parlance of the Fifth Amendment, "compelled" to answer questions if (1) the employee subjectively believes that he/she is compelled to give a statement upon threat of loss of job; and (2) the employee's belief is objectively reasonable at the time the statement is made."

In today's day and age with use of force so "under the microscope", is it any wonder why an officer would invoke his right to protection against self-incrimination? The "politics of force" as mentioned previously comes with many political pressures and interest groups. In such an environment, officers and the attorneys who represent them must ensure that their rights are protected. I am familiar with a prosecutor's office who for years mishandled interviews of officers after a shooting. The lead prosecutor assigned to these cases was seen doodling during interviews, asking arcane questions and making the statement, "The only time I give Miranda is when I believe there's a problem with the shooting." This became common knowledge and one wonders what the next officer interviewed by her felt when she gave him his Miranda warnings?

Is Miranda even warranted? No, unless it is a "custodial interrogation" in which the suspect (officer) is not free to leave. Why would an officer want to receive Miranda? For "use immunity" as the eminent California Police Defense Attorney Michael Stone has stated. I encourage the reader to further educate himself about police officers and the Fifth Amendment by reading Stone's "Taking the Fifth" series I, II, III, IV and V as well as a paper written after the Supreme Court's 2009 decision in the case *Spielbauer v. County of Santa Clara*. Fortunately for us Michael Stone's writings on these topics are available online through www.rcdsa.org (click on the Legal Defense fund then Training Bulletins link).

To quote attorney Stone, "The involved officers' decision to invoke his right against self-incrimination will likely constitute the single, most profound development in the global view of the use of force incident. For example, that single decision removes the statements of the involved personnel who are targeted for prosecution instantly from the reach of the criminal justice system. While compelled accounts based upon pain and penalty of insurbordination are usable in an administrative context, and perhaps in a subsequent civil action, "use immunity" attaches to the statement, precluding its use *for any purpose* in a subsequent criminal case, absent waiver."

Lethal Force and Law Enforcement Activity-Related Deaths —
A Suggested Protocol for Investigation (Michael P. Stone, Esq, 1999,
Legal Defense Trust Training Bulletin, Vol. II, Issue No. 5)

Stone's formula for "use immunity" in statements is:

INVOCATION OF FIFTH AMENDMENT PRIVELEGE (Against self-Incrimination)	+	ADMINISTRATIVE COMPULSION (Insubordination)	=	USE IMMUNITY

("*Taking the Fifth*" Part III, Legal Defense Trust Training Bulletin,
June 1998, Vol. I, Issue No. 3)

Can Garrity be implied? Based on the circumstances, yes it can. In the case we mentioned earlier officers were told they were not free to leave until they completed the mandatory use of force reports they were ordered to write.

My experience and thoughts on the matter are that by including a mandated Miranda or "advised of their constitutional rights" during a use of deadly force or serious use of force incident, you make it easier for an officer to invoke his "right to remain silent" and remove the stress when an officer is given/advised of his 5th Amendment rights. The stress of which I speak is the fact that every police officer who gives a suspect his Miranda Rights knows that any statement, "will be used against him."

An agency must decide if the officer invokes his right to remain silent whether they want to force the officer to make a Garrity statement. Some agencies will say, "We will never compel a statement under Garrity." In some agencies or areas, union representatives will sometimes state, "Never make a voluntary statement."

According to Michael Stone if an outside agency is investigating a use of force such as a shooting, they do not have the authority to "order an officer to make a statement under threat of discipline." Therefore if "use immunity" is sought, it must be the officer's own agency who compels the statement.

Thrown into the mix are prosecutors who will state, "If they won't make a statement, we'll just subpoena them into the Grand Jury." This is a rather curious track for a prosecutor to make in my opinion. I'm aware of a case in which this was threatened against a hero police officer who stopped a mass shooter after he had already killed several innocent victims. Why would a prosecutor be reluctant to offer limited immunity to an officer involved in such a shooting? The way it has been explained to me, "The prosecutor feels that a defense attorney can cast aspersions with a jury about any testimony taken with limited immunity. The prosecutors feel it makes their case harder than it needs to be especially if everyone knows the officer did nothing wrong. Why does the officer need the protection of limited immunity? The prosecutor believes the officer must be hiding something."

What to do? These are issues that must be determined now, prior to an event, rather than in the immediate aftermath of an OIS or death in custody. These decisions should not be made when interested parties (prosecutors, management, investigators and labor) are stressed, tired and emotions running hot.

Somewhere therein is a middle ground based on: the dynamics of the incident, political ramifications, community attitude or tenor, the "politics of force" based on prior incidents; and the treatment of officers by the agency or prosecutor in the past.

By waiting a minimum of 24 hours, up to 72 hours until conducting the interview investigators will have an idea of what actually happened, based on other witness statements — suspect(s) and observers and the physical evidence as well as can have conducted a walkthrough of the scene. In this way the detectives have a feel for the case and can complete a more thorough investigation.

That said if an officer invokes his right to remain silent and/or is forced to make a Garrity statement the criminal investigators and prosecutors or district attorneys and their investigators must leave the interview room. Simply stated, the criminal investigators and prosecutors cannot build a "Chinese wall" in their brain to separate where the information came from (independent investigation or compelled Garrity statement). The only people that should conduct the investigation are internal affairs investigators (that could be detectives assigned to I.A. or in smaller agencies the Chief or his designee who is handling the internal investigation) because the compelled statement can only be used in an internal investigation.

In a perfect world a cooperative statement given of free will by the involved officer to investigators is the way to go because A) He didn't do anything wrong and has nothing to hide, and B) The investigators are from the same agency, and the prosecutors are only interested in supporting an officer who did the right thing and everyone is looking out for the officer's welfare. But that's a perfect world and sometimes not a "real or realistic" world where outside politics and forces come into play. Too many officers have been thrown under the bus by supervisors or agencies to serve political gains or self-interests. Want to see a perfect example of this? Read *13 Minutes* by R. Blaine Jorg (R. Blaine Jorg, unknown date). This officer was abandoned by his agency, charged and tried for involuntary manslaughter in the in-custody death of a suspect. He was subsequently acquitted in a jury trial. I strongly recommend the book for a realistic look at the politics of force at their worst. I have worked on numerous cases where officers did the right thing, operated within agency policy and used an objective reasonable amount of force, only to be charged with crimes by their own agency. This is most often the result of inept investigators and flawed or political investigations.

The last point on this section is that I would strongly suggest that an officer NEVER make a statement (written or otherwise) in a shooting investigation or death of a suspect in custody without an attorney representing him being present. Further, I would recommend that a specialty attorney with experience in such matters be retained by the police union for these events. Having dealt with several different attorneys in these types of investigations, I can state that many have no idea what Garrity is or how it applies or do not understand the scope of an officer involved shooting. Having the right counsel present to protect the officer's rights is vital for *everybody*.

OFFICER INVOLVED DEATH OR SERIOUS BODILY HARM POLICY

I've mentioned that I believe an officer involved death or serious bodily harm policy should be separate from a use of force policy. The reason is that it reduces the overall size and scope of the use of force policy and focuses that policy on the important issues of the use of deadly and non-deadly force and reporting.

The reason an "Officer Involved Death or Serious Bodily Harm Policy" is vital is that there are many instances or incidents outside of a police involved shooting where a full specialty investigation is required and the officer's rights as well as the agency's interests should be protected.

There have been several cases: suspects killed in a motor vehicle accident during a police pursuit, in-custody death involving a subject experiencing excited delirium, or death in-custody at the jail. All of these incidents should be handled by the Officer Involved policy.

The policy should encompass the following parameters, *"The Detective Bureau is responsible for the prompt and thorough investigation of incidents involving an officer acting in an official capacity who uses force that causes or could have caused serious injury to any person, or is the victim of any person who causes or attempts to cause serious injury, or has a person in custody who dies. This policy covers these incidents whether they are accidental, intentional, on duty, off duty, or criminal."*

Sections of the policy include the following procedures:

- Initial patrol response
  - Render the scene safe and account for all possible suspects and victims. After the suspects are secured or known to have left the scene, render first aid and request medical assistance as needed
  - Render the scene secure. Preserve the evidence by securing witnesses, establishing a crime scene perimeter, and initiate the crime scene log. Limit entry into the scene to those responsible for providing first aid and investigators assigned to the case
  - Provide the initial assessment to responding officers, supervisors, and detectives
- Patrol Supervisor
  - If an officer requires immediate transport for medical treatment, assign another officer to accompany him. Suspects and witnesses transported for medical treatment should be accompanied by officers, if possible, or officers should be assigned to the hospitals as soon as possible.
  - Make an initial determination on the size, number and locations of the crime scenes. Secure the crime scenes with tape. Limit access to investigators, and ensure the crime scene log is kept
  - Notify the commander in charge of the patrol shift
  - Sequester the officer(s) involved, if possible, until they have done a walk-through with investigators. Involved

officers should be teamed up with another officer with whom they are comfortable

- ○ Unless there is evidence (fingerprints, blood, etc that may be lost) it is not necessary to immediately seize the officer's weapon
- ○ It is advisable to have the involved officer transported to a local hospital for evaluation. Some injuries have been missed on scene and officers maybe experiencing unhealthy blood pressure or heart-rate issues that can be diagnosed preventing a possible stress induced heart attack or stroke
- ○ Brief responding supervisors and investigators
- Patrol shift commander's responsibilities
  - ○ Ensure crime scene security
  - ○ Assign patrol officers as needed to assist investigators
- Response by on duty Detective Bureau personnel
  - ○ On duty Detective will notify ranking on duty detective supervisor
  - ○ Detective supervisor will make detective bureau assignments
  - ○ Patrol officers and supervisors will brief detectives arriving on scene
  - ○ The DB supervisor on scene will decide if and when the officer's firearm should be taken. The on-scene detective will insure that an inspection is made for the number of rounds for all magazines from the officers directly involved whether they fired or did not fire
  - ○ Assess the need for a search warrant to complete the processing of the scene(s)
  - ○ DB investigators will conduct a walk-though with the officer involved. This walk-though will be confined to a general briefing of what transpired prior to and during the incident. Detectives may ask questions, but more detailed questions will be reserved for the subsequent interview. One union representative and/or union attorney shall be on scene to observe the walk-through. This is not meant to be an interrogation but rather an opportunity for the investigating detectives to more efficiently investigate and document the incident. Care should be taken not to

cause undue stress to the involved officer or to further contaminate the scene. Walk-throughs will not be recorded or filmed

- o Determine if the original taped off area is sufficient to insure that evidence is not lost or contaminated. Consider an adjacent area for media and officials. Request and direct crime scene personnel.
- o Determine additional personnel requirements and factors to consider which include, but are not limited to:
  - The number of scenes to investigate and process.
  - The number of officers, suspects, and victims involved.
  - The number of witnesses to interview.
- o Ensure that the DB commander have been notified and briefed.
- o Crime scene sketches shall be completed at every scene.
- Notifications
  - o If an officer suffers an injury that requires treatment at a hospital, the patrol shift commander will determine if the injured officer is able to notify his family. If the injured officer is unable to make the notification, the shift commander will cause the family to be notified and arrange for the transportation of a spouse, friend, or family member to the hospital.
  - o The Chief of Police will be notified at the appropriate time.
  - o The next series of notifications include:
    - Police Legal Advisor
    - County Prosecutor or District Attorney
    - Police Public Information Officer
    - Union President or his designee
  - o The following should be notified and granted access to the scene once it is released by investigators.
    - Internal Affairs
    - Civil Liabilities
    - Training Bureau Subject Matter Expert
    - Police Chaplain
- Responsibility for the investigation
  - o The ranking DB supervisor

- Will provide a smooth transition and liaison between shifts.
- Provide supervisors from the next shift with a full briefing of the incident and status of the investigation
- Provide a draft copy of the incident report
  - ○ Homicide or Crimes Against Persons Unit
    - Coordinate and direct the continuing investigation and flow of information
    - Provide updated information to the chief, deputy chiefs, investigators on all shifts, and the Public Information Officer, as needed
- Investigation procedures
  - ○ Interview of the involved officer(s) will be scheduled and conducted by the Homicide or Crimes Against Persons Unit detectives. The interview should occur after 24 hours but within 72 hours of the incident, if possible
  - ○ The involved officer shall be provided a union shift representative, advised of their constitutional rights, and have access to counsel prior to and during questioning. The officer may cooperate with the criminal investigation, however, they are under no legal requirement to do so. Interviews of involved officers should be tape-recorded
- Investigation of officer involved incidents requested by other law enforcement agencies within this jurisdiction
  - ○ The on duty commander will respond to the scene and notify the DB commander or his designee
  - ○ The DB commander, or his designee, will determine if this procedure should be activated
- Officer Support Services
  - ○ The Chief's office will contact a member of the Critical Incident Stress Management (CISM) Team to make arrangements for a stress debriefing.
  - ○ All officers involved in an incident involving serious injury or death will attend a mandatory counseling session with a CISM Team counselor. (Agencies should check with their legal advisors on whether these conversations are confidential in their jurisdiction. If they are not, care must be taken as to note-taking or scope of the discussions)

- o The Chief of Police may place the involved officer on administrative leave, with pay, pending completion of the investigations. During such leave, the officer will remain available, unless specifically excused by the Chief of Police
- Firearms inspections
  - o In any firearms discharge in which the involved officer believes that a malfunction of the weapon or ammunition contributed to the discharge, the weapon and ammunition involved will be secured in its present condition immediately following the discharge, without any further functioning of the weapon or removal of ammunition. If the weapon has allegedly malfunctioned, it should be treated as evidence
  - o The weapon should be secured
  - o Upon receipt of the weapon, a certified department armorer will examine the weapon to determine if any malfunction exists. The weapon will be test fired before it is returned to the officer

USE OF DEADLY FORCE INVESTIGATIONS

"When I first started working with police officers involved in shootings there were things I began to notice right off the bat even though I really didn't know a whole lot about police operations. As I would talk to many officers involved in these events, follow them through the investigations, follow them through the media response and the community questions some things became clear one is that we were expecting these events to defy the laws of physics. We were expecting these officers to defy the limits of human performance. We often expect them to have a perfect memory and make perfect decisions when in fact research clearly shows that human beings are not capable of either one of those things. That the training and the judging of police officers is frequently based on myths, assumptions and personal opinions that necessarily may not be true."

Dr. Alexis Artwohl, Lane County I.D.F.I.T.
(Interagency Deadly Force Investigation Team) video,
Lane County, Oregon District Attorney's Office

🗁 CASE STUDIES:

An officer is locked in a suspect holding room (cell without bars) at the station waiting for investigators to interview him after he is forced to shoot an armed robber.

An officer who was just forced to shoot an armed offender is forced to sit in the same room as the Chief of Police and Union President stand toe to toe yelling at each other about procedure and protocol.

After a shooting on the nightshift, the involved officers are forced to stay at the station for hours until they are finally interviewed by Detectives. When they are finally allowed to leave they've been up for over 24 hours without sleep.

All of these events happened and officers who've just fought *and won* a fight for their very lives have had to endure these circumstances, conditions and treatment by their own agencies. It has been said that the best recruitment tool available for an agency is taking care of the officers already under their employ. In that regard, taking care of the officers involved in a shooting or other serious use of force has significant ripples far beyond the one or two officers involved and can impact an entire agency. Pit administration against police union and destroy trust and credibility of police management that is not soon or easily repaired.

This section is <u>not</u> about the investigative techniques and protocols of detectives investigating a non-police involved shooting. That is not my specialty or the subject of this treatise. My focus is on the specifics of dealing with an officer involved shooting or in-custody death case involving use of force. In these types of events, there are several different investigations that take place post event. One is the standard fact gathering for the prosecutor's office to ascertain the legal issues or lawfulness of the police actions and use of force. ★Some jurisdictions have prosecutors or district attorneys with investigators working for them with full police powers. How these investigators integrate with the agency's own detectives is subject to agreements, protocols and policy.

This investigation will be handled by standard homicide investigators from your agency or possibly by a county or state investigative agency if a mutual agreement has been worked out prior. (★This is oftentimes the case for small municipal, village or township agencies that lack the manpower and expertise to investigate an officer involved shooting. Since we've already addressed Garrity it should be mentioned that an investigator from an outside agency *cannot* compel a statement from an involved officer via Garrity. It would take a supervisor from within the officer's agency to make that happen).

This type of investigation requires that the detectives have special knowledge about use of force. After all, what their conclusion in a good shoot will be is justifiable homicide within the law. This goes beyond the standard murder or homicide investigation.

In some locales officers involved in the use of deadly force are called into the Grand Jury for testimony and it is the involved officer's statement as well as the investigators and witnesses who provide evidence to the Grand Jury for them to determine whether the shooting was justified (within the law) or not. Police attorney Mike Stone has an excellent report on officers testifying in front of Grand Juries titled *"Taking the Fifth" – Part IV: When the Grand Jury Requests the Pleasure of Your Company* (Michael P. Stone, P.C. Lawyers; Training Bulletin; Vol. IV, Issue No. 3) which is worth reading for officers as well as supervisors, union heads, investigators and administrators.

Some agencies conduct internal investigations at the same time as the criminal investigations. These investigations focus on whether the officer followed or violated department policies and procedures. Other agencies wait to conduct an internal investigation until after the criminal investigation has been completed and then use the investigative package of the criminal investigators to ascertain if the officer's actions were within rules, regulations and policies.

Let me state that it is vital that the agency maintain control over the investigation. Letting non-investigatory personnel from the local prosecutor's office "run the show" or conduct the interviews, for instance, is fraught with the potential for disaster. Ideally following the agency chain-of-command structure, the highest ranking supervisor in the detective bureau homicide or crimes against persons section should oversee the scene and process as well as handle the interview.

Past mistakes in the way police administrations and detectives investigated these incidents include viewing the officer as the "suspect" in a homicide instead of viewing him or her as the "victim" of a potential murder or felonious assault. This is an important paradigm change. In many cases it is true that investigators would not treat citizen "victims" the same way they treat officer "victims." Sad in my opinion, that we victimize our own officers oftentimes in this process.

It is certainly true that there are elements of the police administration, city or county management, media and citizen groups who feel that any police shooting is a "failure." In other words, something must have gone wrong in order for a police officer to shoot a suspect. What is entirely true on the other hand is that in most shootings *everything went right*. The police officer was confronted with a deadly threat and used deadly force to neutralize or stop that threat against them.

Several years ago I was asked to speak to a local citizen group on police use of force. After my presentation I was approached by an "interesting" gentleman who asked me, "How many people are shot and killed by police officers in this country each year?" While I didn't know the answer off-hand at the time, I responded that "Many more officers are confronted each year by suspects they could have shot and chose not to." He muttered something about conspiracies and walked away but the question left me wondering.

According to Federal Bureau of Investigation on justifiable homicides by police for the period 2006 – 2010:

- The high year was 2009 with (414), the low year was 2008 with (378) homicides by police.
- The numbers as reported by the FBI are: 2006 (386), 2007 (398), 2008 (378), 2009 (414), 2010 (387).
- The 414 justifiable homicides by police in 2009 was the first time this number exceeded (400) since 1994.
- Over the last 30 years, the high year was 1994 with (462) subjects killed by police.

(FBI, Uniform Crime Report, 2010)
http://www.fbi.gov/about-us/cjis/ucr/crime-in-the-u.s/2010/
crime-in-the-u.s.-2010/tables/10shrtbl14.xls

The good thing is that for most agencies serious uses of force as well shootings are infrequent. Some agencies never experience an officer involved shooting. That is the bad thing as well – agencies do not have a "system," protocol or fluid policy and are forced to "wing it" which can damage the process and the officers involved.

That said the idea is to plan, prepare and work out in advance the protocol and system with the parties that will be involved. Interested parties are: legal, agency, and union. The legal interests are usually served by the county prosecutor's office or district attorney. Agency interest is provided by two different groups – criminal investigators and internal affairs investigators. Union protection for the officer will be in two forms: the labor side protecting the officer's rights as an employee, and the legal side which will be provided by a union attorney protecting the individual officer's legal rights.

Without a blueprint on how to proceed some terrible things can happen – to the investigation and also to the officers involved. Here is a "for instance."

🗁 CASE STUDY:

Officer Jones is involved in a shooting. Prior to Homicide Detectives arriving on scene, he is spirited away to the station. The detectives spend 45 minutes looking for cartridge cases in an area where the shooting did not even take place. An Assistant County Prosecutor comes in and in a hurry to get to a social function completes the interview with the primary investigators still out at the scene. The officer is released and leaves the station before the investigators even return to the building.

Based on the above compilation scenario (all true by the way), I would recommend the following:

- Unless injured, the involved officer(s) remain on the scene until debriefed by detectives
- They can be "partnered up" with another officer to stay with them and see to their needs. This may mean having them sit (in the front seat) of a patrol unit
- Unless there is evidentiary reasons, such as blood, physical matter from the suspect (such as from a close proximity

shooting or attempted/actual gun takeaway, fingerprints, etc.) the officer can maintain control of his firearm on scene. If firearms need to be removed the investigator or supervisor should see to it that the officer feels safe, is with another officer or is provided with a replacement firearm

- Once investigators are in place and in the presence of union representation (either shift rep, union leadership or union attorney), the involved officer(s) brief the detectives on what transpired

BRIEFING SUPERVISORS AND RESPONDING DETECTIVES

Involved officer's on-scene statements to investigators has been the subject of some interest in agencies since the Rodney King case. David Hatch writes in his excellent book, *Officer Involved Shootings and Use of Force: Practical Investigative Techniques* (CRC Press, 2003):

> "As a result, police departments and unions developed an "us versus them" attitude that was not the answer to the negative perceptions of law enforcement agencies prevalent then. In an effort to prevent violations of the civil rights of suspects, inmates, and officers and restore agency reputations, several police departments, unions, and other organizations developed administrative warnings for use in cases involving violence."

The following supervisor's warning, Los Angeles Police Department is provided by Hatch:

> "Officer, I am ordering you to give me a public safety statement. Due to the immediate need to take action, you do not have the right to wait for representation before answering these limited questions.

1. In what direction did you fire pistol rounds?
2. If you know of anyone who was injured, what is his or her location?
3. If any suspects are outstanding, what are their descriptions?
4. What was their direction of travel?

5. How long have they been gone?
6. What are they wanted for?
7. What weapons are they armed with?
8. Does any evidence need protection?
9. Where is it located?

> Officer, in order to prevent the contamination of your statement, I order you not to discuss this incident with anyone, including other supervisors or staff officers, prior to the arrival of the assigned investigators, with the exception of your legal representatives."

Somewhere in between a full statement and no statement at all is what we want and the officer must be required to make.

🗁 CASE STUDY:

After a lengthy foot chase of a B&E suspect an officer open fires, wounding the suspect. Investigators follow the path of trajectory and find that an errant round has penetrated the front wall of a home across the street. Checking the house, they find the worst possible outcome, that a citizen has been killed when the bullet struck him in the head.

My opinion is that keeping the officer on scene until investigators arrive, if at all possible, is tremendously beneficial. This is not a "walk-through" per se, but rather the officer, with union representation or legal representation present to protect their rights, briefs the detectives as to the "basics" of what transpired:

> Where is the crime scene?
> Where were you standing or located to begin with?
> Where was the suspect(s)?
> If you moved, in what direction or to what location/position?
> Was the suspect moving? In what direction or to where?
> What direction were shots fired by you and/or the suspect?
> What and where is the evidence?
> Did the suspect touch you, your uniform or your firearm?
> Briefly, what happened?

These questions allow the detective to ascertain what area encompasses the crime scene, where evidence is located and a brief statement of what transpired so they know where and what fact and evidence gathering is necessary to begin with.

The union shift representative or attorney is standing by to prevent a full interview from taking place on scene.

A "walk-through" is a more detailed interview/briefing by the involved officer(s) to investigating detectives. Of course we are not talking about actually walking through (contaminating) the actual scene but rather "walking" the detectives through the incident events. There has been some comment that this may actually cause more emotional trauma to the officer(s). I think that this should be examined on a case by case basis.

Researchers (Dr. Alexis Artwohl and others) have stated that these types of "walk-through" are beneficial in enhancing officer's recollections and memories of the incident.

OIS (OFFICER INVOLVED SHOOTING) INVESTIGATIVE TRAPS

- Treating involved officers like suspects
- Attempting to interview officers prior to a scene walk-through
- Expecting involved officers to have total recall
- Expecting multiple officers to have identical perceptions of events
- Failing to ensure that what the officers and witnesses say happened could have happened
- Failing to view the scene from the officers' and witnesses' vantage points
- Failing to recognize that involved parties may have been in motion during the incident
- Dwelling on why the officer chse a particular course of action rather than another
- Failing to check dispatch tapes, MDT messages and logs
- Including policy opinions in criminal investigation report
- Allowing external influences to rush the investigation

- Mixing the criminal and administrative functions and issues
- Failing to have the involved officer(s) read the final reports before they are approved and submitted

Doyle T. Wright, Public Agency Training Council, 2002

THE OFFICER INVOLVED INTERVIEW

As I have already mentioned, much damage can be done to the officer involved and the investigation if the interview is not conducted properly.

According to James Wilson, Esq.; Edward Geiselman, PhD; and Alexis Artwohl, PhD:

> "It is important to remember that officers involved in shootings are simultaneously 1) subjects who could potentially face criminal indictment, 2) employees who were just doing their jobs but will now be subjected to internal investigations that can put their jobs on the line, 3) witnesses to crimes committed by suspects who attempted to harm the officers and/or citizens, and 4) victims of violent crimes committed by suspects.

> The involved officers therefore play a unique role in the criminal justice system and it is justified to develop specialized procedures in dealing with them to ensure that they are provided with fair, neutral, and objective investigations. The fact that officers and agencies are at risk for becoming embroiled in political controversy as a result of a shooting, no matter how justified the use of force, is another factor calling for specialized procedures that maximize the accuracy, thoroughness, and timeliness of the investigations and any statements provided by the officers.

> An adversarial relationship between the investigator and the involved officer can be created or exacerbated by any tendency by the investigator to handle the interview of a "subject" officer more from a perspective of one conducting a suspect

interrogation than one conducting a witness interview. In that regard, it is crucially important that use-of-force investigators be trained to recognize that officers who have been involved in an OIS are <u>not</u> suspects in any wrongdoing (unless and until evidence of wrongdoing has been developed), but rather are professionals who have been trained, equipped, and sent out onto the street to deal with "critical incidents" on society's behalf, and who have just personally witnessed and experienced such an incident."

(A Good-Practice Approach to Officer-Involved Shooting Investigations; Wilson, Geiselman & Artwohl)

WHEN TO INTERVIEW

There is absolutely no reason that the interview should be conducted in the hours right after the shooting. *Although we are focusing on shootings, suspect death in-custody or major incidents, even a violent encounter involving non-deadly force can be traumatic for officers and leave them feeling exhausted, possibly injured, and in no shape to write a use of force report or make a statement to a supervisor.

There is sufficient scientific evidence to support the notion that waiting for the officer to burn off the stress chemicals such as epinephrine and norepinephrine and engage in a couple of sleep cycles improves memory.

The setting for the interview should never be a room used to interview suspects. A conference room or some safe and comfortable area is the best location.

WHO CONDUCTS THE INTERVIEW?

Understanding that this is a fellow officer and not a criminal suspect may change who conducts the interview. If the supervisor or the detective's demeanor or abrasive style is such that they have the ability to "tick off the Pope himself" another investigator may be a better choice. In small agencies it may be one of the two or both of the detectives available. From my own experience, it only makes sense that an investigator of supervisory rank is in charge of the interview. They have the rank and authority to make things happen and order compliance from subordinates within the interview (I don't mean the officer involved here, I am referring to subordinate investigators and others) and can assign tasks and oversee the investigation.

Present for the interview should be: the primary supervisor investigator, a secondary investigator, an attorney from the prosecutor's office, the police legal advisor, the involved officer and his attorney.

Policy should dictate that a trained investigator (a detective supervisor or detective from that agency or from another who is assigned the case) is the one who conducts the interview. Although others may ask for clarification in the statement later, the primary should be allowed to conduct the interview uninterrupted. When prosecutors or others who are not trained and skilled interviewers are allowed to take control, bad things can result including the officer feeling angry and alienated.

Whether Miranda is given, the statement compelled under Garrity or a voluntary non-Miranda statement made, all of these issues should be worked out prior based on negotiations between the labor and management. Arguments or confrontations should not take place in front of the involved officer.

TYPE OF INTERVIEW

As mentioned earlier in the quote from Wilson, Geiselman & Artwohl a different type of interview than those used in suspect interrogations is recommended. The authors are advocates of the Cognitive Interview style which is further recommended in the report *Guidelines on Memory and the Law* published (and available online) from The British Psychological Society (June 2008). That report cites the British P.E.A.C.E. model for interviewing:

- **Preparation and Planning:** Interviewers are taught to properly prepare and plan for the interview and formulate aims and objectives.

- **Engage and Explain:** Rapport is established with the subject, and officers engage the person in conversation.
- **Account:** Officers are taught two methods of eliciting an account from the interviewee:
  - **Cognitive Interview:** used with cooperative suspects and witnesses.
  - **Conversation Management:** recommended when cooperation is insufficient for the cognitive interview techniques to work.
- **Closure:** The officer summarizes the main points from the interview and provides the subject with the opportunity to correct or add information.
- **Evaluate:** Once the interview is finished, the information gathered must be evaluated in the context of its impact on the investigation.

"The Cognitive Interview includes the following components that focus upon using basic principles in memory and cognition:

Developing rapport: The PEACE model outlines that interviewers should establish ground rules at the beginning of the interview to protect again vulnerability to suggestion, including telling the witness that they should feel free to ask questions when they do not understand, that they should not guess, and that they should tell the interviewer if the interviewer has misunderstood the answer.

Witness participation: Encouraging the witness to actively volunteer information by asking open-ended-questions, refraining from interrupting the witness and encouraging the witness to take a dominant role in the interview conversation.

Context reinstatement: Interviewers instruct the witness to mentally re-state their thoughts, feelings and physical experiences at time of the witnessed event.

Report everything: Asking the witness to report everything they can think of, even if it seems trivial.

Varied recall: Asking the witness to recall the event from a variety of different temporal orders, for example, starting at the end and recalling backwards from there. This aims to minimize the degree to which the witness reconstructs their memory for the event by using their knowledge and assumptions to 'fill the gaps' in their memory.

Imagery: Imagery techniques may be used to probe a witness's mental image of a specific part of an event.

Social dynamics: The Cognitive Interview also includes social techniques at improving interviewer–witness communication.

🗁 CASE STUDY:

From my own experience in an OIS, I can state that I had more than a passing knowledge of the stressful nature of an interview. With my attorney present in a room full of old friends, I gave my statement. As I got lost in the moment telling my "story," I told the investigators and others present about hearing an old partner of mine yell, "I'm hit!" after the shots were fired. Even though I knew that he was okay, I still got emotional retelling the events. If, despite my knowledge of use of force law as well as the effects of stress on the human body, can get emotional when making a statement during an OIS investigation, it goes to show you the dynamics involved.

INVESTIGATIVE CONSULTANTS OR AIDS: USE OF SUBJECT MATTER EXPERTS

The investigator must make use of all the tools and persons at his disposal in a use of force investigation. Most detectives or investigators have a working knowledge of police use of force but not specific expertise in such things as: use of force policy, law, firearms, tactics, dynamics of police shootings, perceptual distortions, sympathetic nervous system reactions, excited delirium and more. Why not take advantage of agency or area experts?

For instance, a shooting may "look bad" because an officer fired at a suspect in a vehicle who was driving away from him. In reality when you examine the process of "response time": (remember the combination of the mental process of "reaction time" coupled with "movement time" – the time between the beginning and end of the physical acts) it is entirely possible that the officer perceived a deadly threat as the vehicle was coming toward him (perception of threat), made the conscious decision to act (reaction time), started shooting and then perceived the threat was no longer there and stopped shooting (movement time). During that process 1) The officer can fire a fairly large number of shots, and 2) The vehicle can travel, depending on its speed, a significant distance. So an officer may be telling the truth as to perceiving a threat through the front windshield and yet having all his hits strike the rear of the vehicle.

📂 CASE STUDY:

I was consulted by a prosecutor in a homicide case many years ago. The case involved the president of a local outlaw motorcycle club who claimed self-defense in a shooting outside the clubhouse during a party. An individual who was kicked out of the party went to his car, came back and threatened the president with a small baseball bat (the kind that baseball teams used to give out on "bat day"). The president claimed he was in fear of his life and got an M-1 carbine from behind the bar and shot his assailant. The immediacy of the attack was a large part of his defense.

The prosecutor's office asked for my assistance reference the time frames and shooting issues of the case. In other words, could it have happened the way the defendant claimed? I took a measuring wheel to the clubhouse and recorded the distance from the outside location of the shooting to the bar area where the gun was kept (the far end of the club). Taking a carbine to the range, I recreated the distance and circumstances, recorded the times involved using a PACT shooting timer (a digital timer which records the audio sound of shots fired). I ran the drill five times and gave my results to the prosecutor who used my testimony to refute the testimony of the defendant and the defense case of a sudden acquisition of a firearm to save his life. The defendant was found guilty of the charges. Hardly TV's C.S.I. and not close to being high-tech but it helped send a murderer to prison.

Since that time, I have been consulted or given testimony in a goodly number of misdemeanor and felony cases involving police use of force or criminal trials of suspects involving force or firearms. I have testified both for and against officers. As a proud member of the profession it saddens me to testify against a brother in blue, but if they are guilty of violations of policy or law then it is my responsibility to be honest and protect my profession and my brothers and sisters in uniform.

Most agencies have subject matter experts in the area of police training, force, shooting and the dynamics of police armed encounters. It only makes sense for an agency (investigators and supervision) to consult with their own experts during the investigation process. Without consulting their experts, the worst of all outcomes, an incorrect one, can be made. Officers have been fired or charged with crimes when a consultation or an investigation by a use of force expert could have vindicated or explained the acts of the officer.

In an internal investigation it is vital that the question, "Did the officer do as they are trained to do?" be answered by the training staff.

Training personnel should have the best knowledge base within the agency of what the "best practices and standards" are in law enforcement (they should have been training along those lines).

Make full use of your agency's resources. Complete a professional and thorough investigation. Consult with your own experts or those outside your agency. If they agree with you their assessment has added another layer of checks and balances. If they disagree with you, find out why and re-examine the case based on their conclusions. Ensure for the officer(s) involved as well as the agency and community that the use of force investigation was properly completed and not based on poorly informed opinion which will not survive a close inspection.

INVESTIGATIVE CONSULTANTS OR AIDS: VIDEO

"Use of force is like making sausage. Even when it's done properly, it still doesn't look good."

Ed Nowicki (Chicago PD ret.,
legendary trainer and founder of ILEETA)

📂 CASE STUDY:

Officers are captured on a gas station video surveillance system apprehending what we are later told is a suspect in possession of a stolen car. The suspect, who is handcuffed behind his back, is leaned over the trunk of a police patrol unit. All of a sudden one of the police officers is seen to reach over and punch the suspect in the face/head area.

Two of the officers involved are disciplined. The officer who punched the suspect lost his job. During the disciplinary hearing we find out that not captured on video was the suspect, though handcuffed behind his back, reaching back and grabbing the officer's testicles. The officer was forced to punch the suspect to get him to let go. The officer was reinstated, but subsequently sued and won sizable damages against the agency.

Since the Rodney King video and into the YouTube age, we have been inundated with police use of force videos. But what we see is often not the whole story and the two dimensional aspect of video can distort the "facts." We should never make a decision on a use of force based strictly on the visual image provided by video.

It's interesting to note that even in the State Court trial of the officers involved in the Rodney King case, Sgt. Charles Duke a legendary L.A.P.D. use of force instructor defended the officers with the tape by breaking the video down frame by frame. Sgt. Duke testified that only reasonable force was used against King. Regardless of your opinion on that case, my point is that videos of use of force incidents that look bad may in fact be completely reasonable.

📂 CASE STUDY:

In Chapter Six we examined the case of Officer Charlie who was indicted by the local county prosecutor for Felonious Assault in the officer involved shooting of a suspect who attempted to rob a department store where the officer was working off-duty. I stated that the indictment was based in large part on a video tape of the incident captured by the store's security camera in the parking area.

The video segment viewed by the prosecutor and the grand jury and used to indict him shows the officer attempting to tackle a suspect that is running away. The suspect seems to break the tackle and get some distance away when the officer raises his pistol and appears to fire causing the suspect to stop running and hobble toward a car parked in the lot where he is taken into custody.

Because no quality interview was ever generated by the investigators in the case no one ever asked Charlie's version of the events. Had they, they would have reported that the suspect had tried to disarm the officer in the store prior to the shooting and that this incident was actually one large violent event leading to a series of shots being fired.

Our heavy set officer (close to 400 lbs.) was tossed around by a suspect that was under the influence of Cocaine. Though smaller in stature and lighter in weight the suspect had the strength of "Hulk Hogan" according to the officer. This was backed up by physical evidence (a bent metal detector the two had impacted with prior to entering the vestibule. The officer dropping to his knees and feeling that he was losing a fight for his life with a determined violent robbery suspect draws his handgun and fires twice. One round impacts the suspect's cheek, the other misses. Instead of backing down or giving up, the suspect fights harder throwing our officer with his pistol in hand through a plate glass exit door. Officer Charlie lands on his back with the suspect on top of him. The suspect stands up and aggressively crams his hand into a pants pocket (a metal crack pipe would later be found in the pocket). Our officer continues shooting three more times with one of the projectiles shattering the suspect's leg.

When I interviewed the officer in his attorney's office, he told me that the tape the prosecutor and grand jury had seen was not a tape of the shooting. The shooting had taken place prior to the attempted tackle. The point of the video where the prosecutor's office thought the shooting took place was actually when the officer had just raised his pistol and not fired.

I immediately left the interview returned home and downloaded the video. I imported the video into a digital editing program in my computer. The program, which came free with my laptop, allowed me to take a digital photo or still of every frame of the video. Breaking the video down in this matter I was able to determine that there was only 0.4 of one second when the officer had raised his pistol up toward the suspect. Is it physically possible for an officer to raise a pistol from a 45 degree angle downwards to parallel with the ground and fire three shots in 0.4 of a second?

I went to the range and using a PACT Timer was unable to recreate the speed as demonstrated on the video. It took me more than 0.4 of a second just to raise and fire one shot let alone three. Now, during a string of fire manipulating the trigger as fast as I could, I was able to fire a shot about every tenth of a second but not raise and fire within the times indicated.

I immediately reported my findings to the defense team and submitted a written report which vindicated the officer. Soon after, another tape from another surveillance camera (a different angle) was found which actually showed the shooting. In my opinion, viewing the tape you could clearly see the .40 caliber round being fired and shattering the suspect's femur. The shooting, as the officer had stated, occurred before the attempted tackle and well before the tape the prosecutor used to indict the officer. When the county prosecutor dismissed the charges he referred to the defense team's "experts" and newly found evidence when he did the press conference. All I did was apply solid use of force investigative techniques such as: basic interviewing skills, knowledge of use of force law, basics of human movement and shooting, basic video tape editing and an inquisitive mind.

Although this was a "win" for the officer, he went through hell in the interim. Facing a criminal trial he told me that his father had passed away in the time after he was indicted. Sad to think his Father went to his grave not knowing of his son's proven innocence.

It didn't (and shouldn't) have to go this way. A solid investigation by his own agency would have revealed the facts and supported his decision to shoot.

As graphic or seemingly encompassing as video images are on use of force incidents, they are not the *whole picture*. All of the other facts and evidence of a solid investigation must be considered before reaching a conclusion.

Dr. Bill Lewinski from Force Science had this to say about video tapes of police use of force:

> "People tend to think that a video is an accurate reporter of any particular incident. But I would like you to look at the number of cameras that are necessary for referees to look at any football game. The more cameras they have the more angles they can see things from the better their judgment is

about whether or not the action their judging is portrayed accurately and completely. So we know that one video camera from a particular perspective is very limiting in its ability to see anything. Even for instance there's a camera that officers are wearing that sits just in front of the officer's ear. And this reportedly has a view of the officer. It does not. If you close your left eye, for instance, you will see what your right eye sees and your right eye sees a different field of view than your left eye. And your body links both of those. Now imagine you're a camera far behind your right eye, what does that see? It's seeing what's directly in front of the face not even what the right eye is seeing. It really doesn't show the field of view on the left. No camera records things as an officer's eye and brain is recording it that's really embedded in the situation. Just as a quarterback is seeing a different field of view than the viewer sitting at home watching the camera capture the action on the football field."

Dr. Bill Lewinski, Lane County I.D.F.I.T.
(Interagency Deadly Force Investigation Team) video,
Lane County, Oregon District Attorney's Office

The following section is on the types of video tape evidence and problems associated with viewing, downloading, recording and otherwise processing these tapes.

CELL PHONE VIDEO EVIDENCE

Most cell phones are able to capture videos nowadays. An expert in this field told me that he would rather process the actual phone and retrieve the video in that manner versus having a cooperative witness with evidence on his phone send the video to him via email. Although there is no difference in the quality of the video received, it removes one less person in the chain of custody and also allows the tech to retrieve the video evidence in several different ways.

Cheaper pre-paid or other types of phones may have the data ports on the phone disabled and this may not allow the tech to directly download the material. The file on these phones will have to be emailed to the investigator.

Other phones have removable memory cards which allow the file to be sent to, then the card removed and the data directly downloaded onto the investigator's computer (heads up, these micro cards oftentimes require a convertor disk to be directly placed into most laptops or PC's).

A frequently used type of video program for cell phones is 3GP which saves the video as an MPEG (Moving Pictures Experts Group). MPEG files can usually be viewed on most Microsoft® and Apple® based computers. Other types of files may require a different program.

There are several different CODEC (compressor-decompressor or coder-decoder) programs that video files may use. I've run into problems when use of force case Compact Disks or a DVD is delivered to me and upon inserting them into my trusty laptop a window opens up asking me what program I want to use to open the file.

According to my computer/phone expert (thanks Guy...) there is an excellent website www.portableapps.com which allows the user to download an app link to their desktop. Even with agencies with locked computer systems to prevent downloading files, the app can be run allowing different video formats to run. Note – the reader uses and downloads content at their own risk. I can make no guarantees about this or any other website being free from viruses.

SURVEILLANCE VIDEO FOOTAGE

One of those things that must be included in a use of force investigator's checklist is to ask if there are any video cameras present. This may require some work as some systems may be running in closed businesses.

It is important that even after seemingly "minor" use of force incidents video, if available, is captured and placed into evidence. In one case I'm familiar with a jail system may have recorded the incident but the tape segment was not gathered which meant that within a certain amount of time it was recorded over and hence lost forever. This can be costly as the minor incident may end up in court in a civil action.

📁 CASE STUDY:

In one case involving multiple officers (four officers were charged) a security camera at a self storage facility captured the arrest of a fleeing burglary suspect. After the running suspect is clipped by a patrol car he falls to the ground. Four officers stomp or kick the suspect. Four officers were charged with misdemeanor assault in the case and three other officers were fired but not indicted. ★As of this writing one officer fired but not charged has been reinstated. The indicted officers have not yet gone to trial. This video "does not look" good but the "totality of the circumstances is not known so comment will not be made. This case is used as an illustration of how non-police video systems may capture an incident.

There are still VHS video cassette recorders in use in marts, stores, markets and other private business surveillance camera systems in this country although most have moved to digital video. VHS degrades over time but the loss is minimal. Usually systems that incorporate VHS have very large tape sizes and record at very slow speeds as well as reuse their tapes on a regular basis. These older tapes recorded at low resolution or slow speed can cause distortion or the images to appear "scratchy" or "grainy."

Next up on the surveillance video progression is the use of digital mediums such as a CD or DVD. These types of systems offer all the advancements of a movie DVD with a clearer picture and less degradation over time. Detectives can frequently walk out of the business with a CD or DVD ready to view with the original disk or one burned for them by the owner or manager. Note – It has been my experience that nightshift cashiers and employees seldom have "the keys" to access the system after hours or the ability to burn a disk for you. This may require that detectives return the next day to obtain the video or that the manager or owner is called at home and summoned in to provide the video.

Finally, like the advancement of patrol car video systems from VHS to DVD, and now to digital hard-drive type files, surveillance systems have done the same thing. Some are engineered with an attached disk burner which will allow the owner to burn a disk of the captured incident. Some may require that a laptop with the appropriate software be connected to the surveillance system to download the video.

As my video/cell phone/computer consultant has said reference both – cell phone and surveillance system – videos, collection or recording of the incident may require an old way of setting up a camcorder to film the monitor or computer screen. It doesn't usually come out well (based on the TV screen, monitor's display setting) but is better than nothing if agency technology has not caught up with the surveillance or phone video system.

INVESTIGATIVE CONSULTANTS OR AIDS: SPECIFIC LE EVIDENCE

After a serious use of force incident there will frequently be specific evidence left by the officer on scene. For instance there can be the detritus of law enforcement equipment such as dropped citation books, dropped equipment such as a flashlight or specific instruments or evidence of force applications. These can be used to get an idea of the violent nature of the use of force incident and may include badges torn from uniforms, etc. Specific use of force tools can leave behind evidence which may or may not need photographed, collected or at least noted by an investigator. These items may be dropped, sprayed, shot, or ejected and maybe strewn around the scene. These include:

Taser® – When fired Taser AFID™ (Anti-Felon Identification) tags (between 20 to 40) drop to the floor in the area in front of where this ECD was pointed. The location of the tags can be used in incidents where the Taser cartridge has been fired to ascertain location. If two or more Tasers or cartridges have been fired then there will be multiple AFID tags present. Tags can be related to specific cartridges. Taser International would be able to determine which tags belong to which cartridge submitted.

Taser cartridges may have been removed and dropped to the ground if the device was reloaded and another shot fired. Taser training would have officers drop the cartridge versus putting them in a pocket for instance.

That said, newer Taser models such as the X2 or X3 have two or three cartridges respectively. Unless more than these two or three cartridges are fired, they will not be reloaded (and cartridges dropped).

Taser cartridges available have maximum range capabilities of (between 15 and 35 feet). Although each cartridge can fire under its maximum capacity distance, it cannot exceed it. Comparing cartridge range to reported positions can be used to clarify officer/subject positions and locations.

Taser wires will be on the ground usually in a tangled mess. These microfilament wires may or may not be connected to the probes.

Probes are the business end of a Taser cartridge. Probes are small metal cylinders which attach to skin or clothing via sharp metal "fish-hook" style sharpened "probe points." Standard probe point length is 0.38" with the longer probe on the XP (Extra Penetration) cartridges measuring 0.53". Propelled by compressed nitrogen, the probes have a velocity of about 180 feet per second. The maximum spread pattern of any of the Taser cartridges is the 25 foot cartridge which will have an approximate three foot spread at its capacity range. Probes may or may not be attached to the suspect upon the supervisor or investigator's arrival. Standard practice is for EMS to pull the probes out of soft tissue and place a band-aid on the point of impact. Probes may be attached to suspect clothing and if the wires are pulled out may actually still be in/on the clothing at booking or in the Emergency Room if the suspect is transported to those locations. Photos of Taser probe penetration points in skin must be photographed.

A Taser can have the cartridge removed and be used in the "drive stun" mode by an officer shoving the front of the ECD into a suspect. A drive stun can also be used to follow-up in addition to firing the cartridge. At closer distances a standard practice is to fire the cartridge (which is always more effective) and then press the Taser into the person, thereby increasing the size of the "circuit" thus improving effectiveness. The result of pressing a Taser into a person in drive stun mode is what is commonly referred to as "signature marks." These are not burns, but rather the points at which the electricity contacts the subject's skin. Because this is painful and relies on physical contact as well as the dynamics of a resisting arrest or detention encounter, a subject who is being drive stunned will often move. Each time the skin is touched a new set of signature marks are made. In some instances this has been improperly construed as excessive force when the officer states he only used the Taser in drive stun once and yet there are multiple marks on the skin. Several different sets of signature marks can be made during one five second cycle (each pull of the trigger cycles the Taser for five seconds).

The Taser International units can be attached to a computer via a USB cable and with software provided by Taser International each unit's deployment applications can be noted. When a Taser is hooked up to the computer program it can generate a report that will show:

- Serial Number
- Model Number (M26, X26, X2, etc.)
- Date report generated
- Record Date Range (with an option for All Data)
- Recorded Firing Data (Including):
  - Sequence (As in 001 to 0014 applications)
  - Local Date and Time of cycling)
  - Duration of cycling (in seconds)

Chemical Irritant Sprays – The most common type of chemical irritant spray used in law enforcement today is OC (Oleoresin Capsicum) a derivative of pepper products. OC in its purest form is very thick and cannot be sprayed via an aerosol projector unless it is contained within a solvent. Solutions or solvents can include water as well as chemicals such as Trichloroethylene among others. OC may be sprayed by an aerosol projector from a belt carried spray canister. Delivery types of spray include a stream, foam, gel or a cone fog. Streams tend to be more effective against a suspect's eyes which are the primary target. Fogging units are more effective against a suspect's breathing because they are more easily inhaled. Foam or gel units spray out a thicker stickier more highly viscous version of pepper product that is harder to remove from the skin and splashes off target less. When used pepper spray may result in a brownish stain on clothing, walls or light colored surfaces or material may be seen. Splash may occur with OC rebounding or glancing off the target area.

Most OC manufacturers include some type of ultraviolet dye in the product that may still be visible with a black light a day or two after the application. There are newer OC products which may even leave a visible blue stain on the suspect's skin.

Riot Chemicals and Munitions – In a riot situation it is entirely possible that mobile field force members will use force on many people (as in blanketing the area with CS (Chlorobenzalmalononitrile) gas fired from 37 or 40mm gas guns or spraying participants with larger riot size canisters of liquid OC spray. If a riotous crowd has been ordered to disperse based on violations of your state laws then chemical munitions can be used to effectively move them out of an area or deny them an area. Further, non-lethal munitions in the form of sting-ball grenades and impact munitions (12 gauge, 37 or 40mm direct fired impact munitions) can be used from a distance to control rioters or violent offenders within a crowd. These chemicals and munitions can also be used against unruly or rioting prisoners within a jail or prison.

In the case of an outdoor riot, it may be hard to identify those persons who were gassed or struck. Riot control tactics would suggest that police teams would rather drive them from the area than try to arrest everyone. A good tactic for prosecution of criminal cases, identification of those involved and liability protection is to have a police video team(s) record actions prior to, during and after police arrive. A blanket incident and use of force report indicating force application documents those officers involved and the types and nature of force used.

Arrest teams will make hands-on arrests of the worst of the offenders. If those officers use force on a suspect then their picture should be taken with the person arrested and use of force reports completed. This will help identify which officer arrested which subject for processing and reporting purposes.

Riot munitions such as "knee knockers" and rubber sting-balls are designed to be "skip-fired" or bounced off the ground, asphalt or concrete at rioters. Unfortunately the angle that they skip or bounce off the pavement cannot be controlled and they have the capacity to strike rioters in the head or other vital areas.

To better explain what an investigator may be looking at when surveying an urban riot scene and force application, I'll give a "typical" scenario:

A riotous situation erupts after a large fight in a downtown area bar district. Patrol officers pull back with supervisors forming a Mobile Field Force. Riot shields are obtained as are riot chemical munitions. Grenadiers are assigned and supervision assigns line and arrest teams. The entire force dons riot helmets and gas masks and caravans into the area in a show of force. A line of shield carrying officers deploys a block from the rioters. The mobile field force commander gives multiple verbal orders over a portable P.A. system that the crowds must disperse or face arrest. The response is a barrage of beer bottles thrown toward police lines. The commander orders the grenadiers to fire 37mm smoke grenades toward the crowd as a demonstration of force and to check wind direction. This only incites the crowd. Grenadiers are ordered to fire 150 yard CS gas projectiles in front of the crowd. The CS plumes of smoke drift toward the crowd driving many away but hard-core intoxicated rioters persist some even picking up the projectiles and tossing them back toward police lines.

The commander orders the skirmish line to move forward and they do so tapping their batons on the side of their plastic shields to attempt to intimidate the rioters. As they are moving forward multiple 80 yard CS gas rounds are fired in front of the crowd. Coming adjacent to alleyways on their left and right the commander sees suspects hiding in the darkness and orders CS rubber ball grenades tossed into those areas. As the skirmish line nears the rioters a few suspects run into the area in front of the main body of rioters and attempt to throw various missiles at police. They are taken down by less-lethal officers firing ARWEN 40mm projectiles. Arrest teams move through the lines and snatch the arrestees up carrying them back behind the police line. As they near the rioters muzzle blast CS gas is fired directly at the crowd as well as OC spray from large canisters. Some die-hard and drunk rioters are brought down by the arrest teams with strikes from expandable batons as well as the Taser.

The crowd is dispersed and order restored.

The agency must now document its use of force. Evidence to photograph despite any damage done by the rioters will be the detritus of force applications – spent 37mm aluminum casings will litter the scene, any hand thrown gas or rubber ball grenades, projectiles from the ARWEN launcher, Taser AFIDs and more. Specific reports on use of force must be completed by individual officers along with an overall report by the commander.

Facing a media that frequently sees excessive force in every application, you must report and investigate force applied in riot or crowd situations even if that means that Officer Doe sprayed multiple unknown suspects with OC spray outside of Bilbo's Bar on Main St. and they scattered.

If you don't properly document, investigate and report you will have multiple "victims" filing suit and no department evidence to prove your case or defend the agency.

Kinetic Energy Impact Munitions – Also known as bean bag rounds, these ballistic nylon projectiles are filled with lead birdshot and can be fired from 12 gauge shotguns and/or 37 or 40mm launchers. 12 gauge impact munitions came onto the market years ago with a flat square design. Sadly the flat design led the projectile to "Frisbee" or drift off target. This lack of accuracy resulted in greater injury to suspects. Additionally the edges of these bags could lacerate skin and possibly not expand at all striking like a ballistic nylon slug that may penetrate the skin.

Design changes were made and now these impact munitions resemble socks. An average 12 gauge sock type projectile weighs 40 grams and has a velocity at the muzzle of about 280 feet per second.

Striking with the kinetic energy of a Nolan Ryan fastball, these projectiles can be used effectively out to 50 feet or so (at the more extended ranges they are "lobbed" in on target).

In terms of accuracy, ability to hit at distance and disabling impact the 37mm and 40mm projectiles such as the ARWEN or CTS foam baton impact munitions are the most effective non-deadly force application available. These launched projectiles average 100 grams in weight, have a muzzle velocity of 250 feet per second and have the ability to deliver effective force on a suspect at a range of 30 yards. The launcher's barrels for these rounds are rifled which increases accuracy over smooth-bore 37mm gas guns.

Targeting as taught in most impact munitions instructor courses is to large muscle masses, i.e. the outside of the thigh (Common Peroneal Motor-Point), front of the thigh, buttocks, lower abdomen (gut), and the large muscles of the back. Areas to be avoided are over the heart, the throat, face, neck and head as well as groin, areas over the spine and low back (kidney area). Boney areas such as the elbow, wrist, and knee should be avoided if possible as well.

In an ideal word, ideal targets are struck. In the real world, with the dynamics of confrontation (movement & stress for instance or if no other target is available, i.e. a suspect behind cover) a non-ideal target may be struck. This does not make the application unreasonable or "excessive." The question as with all use of force applications is whether the force used was objectively reasonable based on the totality of the circumstances at the moment the "trigger is pulled." Accidental or even secondary injuries (a subject who is hit falls and injures his head) are not the question. The question is whether the force used was reasonable.

Expected injury is limited to bruising which may be quite colorful a couple days after a suspect is struck. Due to the impact energy imparted on target any subject shot with kinetic energy impact munitions should be evaluated by local paramedics for injury and photographed by investigators.

Batons – Traditional wood and polycarbonate batons have given way to metal expandable or tactical batons which are more easily carried and deployed. Traditional targets are listed as: primary – large muscle masses; secondary – joints or bones; and deadly force targets – the head, neck or throat. That said, we must be careful in applying a manufacturers training program for what may be objectively reasonable based on the circumstances.

Once again, ideal targets are suggested. If an officer only has a joint or bone available as a target, is she to refrain from striking a suspect and possibly being injured in the process? In a dynamic situation (a knock-down-drag-out bar fight) it is entirely possible that a baton swung at a large muscle mass may strike an unintended target such as the head. More than a few cops have been hit by a fellow officer's baton or flashlight strikes in these types of situations over the years. It is up to the investigator to determine if the target struck was intentional or not.

Injuries will ideally be limited to bruising but lacerations in the scalp are typical if the head is struck.

Flashlight Impacts – Years ago large aluminum body flashlight were introduced to the police market with the Kel-Lite hitting the market in the 1970's. I carried an 18 inch C-cell Kel-Lite Baton-light while working as a security officer during college. Soon several different C, D or rechargeable aluminum body lights were available to police.

Although they were brighter and sturdier than previous plastic flashlights, the problem with these larger, heavier lights which were used to replace batons is that there was little to any training that took place. Combine a heavier striking tool with little to no training and the result was a lot of head strikes and injuries to suspects (several of whom died as a result). In civil cases against law enforcement agencies plaintiff attorneys would accuse officers of striking their client with a metal pipe. In addition, lacerations with the lights were common because they were not originally designed as impact weapons and switch assemblies would cut the suspects skin during a strike.

Some agencies reacted to the civil liability by prohibiting flashlights to be used by officers as impact weapons. This seems like over-reaction and silly. Once again it sets the stage for an officer's use of force to be perfectly legal but prohibited by policy. Additional this will certainly be brought up against the agency and officer in a civil case resulting in more liability not less. A better answer is to train officers how to hit properly with whatever impact tool is used.

Since that time, developments in LED (Light Emitting Diode) technology as well as advances in plastics and rechargeable batteries, have shrunk the size of the average police flashlight. Though smaller and lighter these lights are brighter than ever. The result has been that flashlights used as batons have been virtually eliminated. (This doesn't mean that there are not instances when a flashlight is in an officer's hand and used to strike or when the officer is attacked while holding the light and lashes out in self-defense striking a suspect.)

As in all use of force investigations it is the responsibility of the supervisor or investigator to sift through the facts of the case and determine whether the flashlight impact was reasonable.

SWAT Specialty Munitions (Chemical and Impact) – Similar to the specialty riot chemicals already covered, SWAT specialty chemical and impact munitions use needs to be documented and investigated. Specialty munitions and devices used by SWAT include: flash-bangs, barricade penetrating chemical rounds, sting-ball, and more.

Flash and Noise Distractionary Devices (FNDD) or Flash-bangs

Flash and Noise Distractionary Devices, also known as Flash-bangs, have become a mainstay of police tactical teams since they were first introduced into the American police market after the Los Angeles Police Department began using them in preparation for the 1984 L.A. Olympic Games.

These devices are constructed of steel with ports on the top and bottom. As an example the Model 7290 from Combined Tactical Systems is Magnesium, Aluminum and Potassium Perchlorate. Upon detonation the FNDD produces a 6 to 8 million candela flash as well as a loud bang (175 db at five feet for the CTS #7290). The flash and noise is combined with a pressure wave increase of approximately 1.63 P.S.I. The pressure, bang and brilliant flash disorients suspects, allowing officers to safely enter houses or rooms, as well as used to distract criminal offenders outdoors allowing team members to more safely take them into custody or apply force by other means (K-9 or impact munitions) for instance.

Early versions of FNDD's were more inclined to cause fires as well "go projectile." (Early designs only had one port on the bottom. If they landed end down or up against a hard surface like a wall they could "shoot up or out" injuring SWAT officers or suspects. I've seen several incidents where officers were injured by the one pound body of the FNDD striking them). Minor burns can result if the device lands on or very close to a suspect.

Newer designs in FNDD's incorporate more vents in both the top & bottom of the body of the device as well as designs that now limit rolling of the flashbang when it's thrown. You will commonly see "scorch" marks on carpeting and linoleum tile to indicate where the device detonated. Since tactical personnel may kick the FNDD body when entering the structure or room the body may actually be found away from the detonation point.

Additionally the metal "spoon" will fall off as the FNDD is let go by the tactical officer during deployment. There will be a separation between the body of the FNDD and this spoon.

Further, because of the odd way the pressure wave may bounce around a structure based on walls and openings, a rear glass window may be blown outward that is nowhere near the detonation point.

FNDD's are explosive devices and a fire may start if the device is tossed into draperies, clothes or other combustible materials or liquids.

Chemical Munitions

In barricade situations where a suspected armed or dangerous suspect is ensconced within a structure, SWAT teams can deploy Ferret® or barricade penetrating chemical munitions rounds. These hard plastic projectiles are normally fired through windows into a structure. Payloads can be micropulverized forms of OC and CS or liquid versions of both chemicals. Standard tactical team deployment would be to fire these projectiles on an angle upward through a window so that the chemicals can drop down onto the suspects in the room(s).

Years ago ICT (Incapacitation Concentration and Time) as well as LCT (Lethal Concentration and Time) would be required to be computed using standards for CS and based on the size of the rooms that the chemicals would be fired into. For instance, if a bedroom ten feet by ten feet with an eight foot ceiling was the target area, the square footage of the room would be entered into an equation combined with the grams of chemical and a standard for CS. SWAT gas teams could then compute how much time it would take for someone in the room to be incapacitated as well as when a lethal level were reached. There was no lethal level for OC.

A number of years ago the National Tactical Officers Association as well as most chemical munitions companies did away with the ICT/LCT concept. This was based on the fact that chemicals are not deployed in closed rooms but rather vented rooms when windows are broken out or doors are open. Further, the LCT concept is moot when the suspect is armed and dangerous and capable of shooting SWAT team members if/when they enter the structure.

Physical evidence of barricade penetrating chemical munitions projectiles for the investigator will be a rounded tip or cap of the projectile (depending on manufacturer design), the plastic projectile (which may be broken or in pieces) and the containing casing (which will be either dropped by the grenadier or tactical gas officer on the ground after firing or retained with him).

Care should be taken when investigating the scene of use of force involving chemical munitions. As mentioned these chemicals can be in micro-pulverized form and may become airborne when walking through the scenes. It is recommended that investigators change clothes or wear coveralls and wear an air purifying respirator (gas mask).

Pepperball®

Although the most common brand name of small liquid or powder OC gas powered projectiles, this category covers a number of different OC ball launchers. Some like Pepperball look very much like paintball "markers" or launchers, others look like M-4 carbines. It may be a .68 caliber ball containing liquid or powder Oleoresin Capsicum or a harder plastic finned projectile like the FN 303®. The FN design based on the barrel rifling of the launcher and the finned launcher are more accurate out to distance whereas the ball projectile are typically used closer in. These designs combine the kinetic energy transference of an impact round with the debilitating nature of pepper spray. It is not unusual for a number of projectiles (over ten) to be fired at a suspect using one of these devices.

In corrections type of deployments where suspects may be hiding underneath their bunks covered with a mattress, it is not unusual for these ball projectiles to be fired into the wall or floor near the inmate to get the air around them contaminated with pepper product.

Evidence on scene of a ball style pepper launcher will be, in addition to talcum like powder on the floor on lying about, small fragments of the biodegradable balls.

DOCUMENTATION BY SWAT OR TACTICAL TEAMS

It is important that SWAT document their use of force incidents. Narcotics search warrants completed by dynamic tactical team entry rely on speed, surprise and violence of action. Suspects inside these locations are quickly and forcefully taken to the ground when orders to get down are ignored. In order to protect officers and the agency as well as provide a report source to defend against unmeritorious litigation suits which can be filed a couple of years after the event with trials occurring as long as four or more years after a use of force incident, investigation and documentation are crucial.

Also, because of the specialized knowledge in best practices and standards of Special Weapons and Tactics operations and equipment it is beneficial if the investigator has been or is on SWAT.

FIREARM CASINGS

📁 CASE STUDY:

Several years ago as a junior patrol officer my partner and I were summoned to an officer involved shooting scene. A supervisor had shot a subject in a car after being threatened with a gun. The suspects fled the scene in the vehicle. Several supervisors were already on scene and we were ordered to complete an incident report for the shooting. The business location was never closed nor was the scene taped off. It was still open with patrons coming and going. At one point after talking to a high-ranking supervisor I heard what sounded like a cartridge casing being kicked by a female customer as she walked through the lot. Fearing that the casing would be lost, I followed the noise with my flashlight and picked up the casing.

Sitting behind the wheel of the patrol car a veteran sergeant approached me and asked if I was the officer who had found the casing?" I replied that I was and was currently in the process of completing the evidence report to tag the casing into evidence. He asked me, "Why wasn't the scene secured?" I told him, "Sarge, I'm not in charge of the scene." He looked over at the three supervisors in the lot and said, "You're right," and walked away.

Ejected casings from firearms are specific evidence that needs to be photographed in place and tagged into evidence. It is, however, impossible to say decisively where exactly an officer was standing when he or she fired rounds from pistols, shotguns, subguns, or carbines. Too many variables come into play such as angle and cant of the gun when fired and movement of the officer. The Force Science Institute under Bill Lewinski, PhD, did a study several years ago on ejection patterns of semi-auto pistols. According to that study, "The results of this study demonstrated how unpredictable spent cartridge casing ejection patterns are even when many variables are controlled. A total number of 7,670 bullets were fired from eight different firearms in the course of this study." Their conclusion: "As this study has shown, factors previously listed including firearm design, firearm condition, ammunition type, position firearm is held when fired, movement of the firearm and person during firing, and grip factors such as how, where and how tightly the firearm is held during firing can affect the locations of spent cartridge casings (Hueske, 2006). This study illustrated that even when accounting for the above factors, significant variability occurred in the landing locations of spent cartridge casings. This variability must be considered before efforts are made to establish the location of a shooter based solely on the location of even an undisturbed spent cartridge casing or a group of cartridge casings." (*Fired Cartridge Case Ejection Patterns From Semi-Automatic Firearms;* Lewinski, Hudson, Karwoski, Redmann, 2010)

POLICE K-9

I'm a big fan of well-trained police canines as trackers of suspects as well as their ability to run after and apprehend a fleeing suspect. Police dogs are an effective means of locating and/or stopping dangerous persons thereby reducing injuries to police officers who without them, would have to engage in risky foot chases or enter and search locations/areas without them.

When a K-9 apprehends a suspect by biting and holding them until they can be taken into custody, it is a police use of force. As such, it needs to be reported and investigated including: photographs, handler use of force reports (this may be in addition to a K-9 Use Report), witness and suspect interviews, etcetera.

In some areas K-9's and their use against suspects is not as favored as others. To maintain the integrity of the K-9 program and protect against accusations of excessive force, a professional training program and documentation is necessary.

MEDIA ISSUES

🗁 CASE STUDY:

A supervisor is involved in a use of force along with a couple of his officers with racial accusations by the "victim's" family. He is asked by the chief of police to take part in a press conference to defend the agency and their actions. When he tells the chief that he is leery to be involved based on his actual participation in the altercation and the civil ramifications, he is told he is not a "team player."

There was a time when agencies were reluctant to speak to the media and "circled the wagons" with a resounding *"no comment."* Such times are now past with most agencies having a trained Public Information Officer (PIO) within the organization. These PIO have contacts and build relationships with the local media. Even if the only official comment from the agency is, "The incident is currently under investigation" it is better than no comment at all. As is said of the media in dealing with police, "You have to feed the beast or it will find something to feed upon." This can include running interviews with anti-police elements in the community that can hurt relationships in the community. As has been said prior, there is a certain group within the community who believe that any shooting or use of force that takes place is a failure. Instead of viewing an officer who was threatened with his own death or serious bodily injury and who used his firearm to stop an attack against him as a victim, they view them as the suspect of an excessive use of force. It seems that many members of the media under the "if it bleeds it leads," philosophy of selling newspapers, luring viewers or listeners will generate controversy by giving air to anti-police groups or individuals. Some unprofessional talking heads on TV or radio as well as print media without having all of the facts or any knowledge of the subject matter, will give traction to all kinds of wild and unsubstantiated rumors or theories.

How many riots, violent marches or negative citizen and police contacts have been generated by the media fanning the flames of controversy? Where are these media types and their coverage, once the investigation is complete and the facts prove that the officers acted properly? Front page media generated controversy is followed up by Page 10 retractions or apologies or news blurbs that officers acted within the law.

That said, the "forth estate" as the media is referred to have an important role and do supply society with checks and balances on police conduct. It is their job to report when excessive force is proven.

Agencies are encouraged to assign and train a PIO. This frees investigators and others in officer involved use of force incidents to focus on doing their job and not be distracted by the media. When talking to the media the PIO must remember to stay on point and topic and not make statements about use of force issues that are not his purview. Although every member of an agency should have a working knowledge of agency use of force policy and use of force law, damage can be done by overstepping your knowledge base.

If more detailed information is sought and the agency believes it is important, training personnel can give interviews. Although detailed questions about the incident should be avoided (and agreed upon in advance with the reporter) basic questions or information about use of force, performance under fight or flight and the like can be covered.

With agency approval, I have given interviews and statements about such topics as Taser use, in-custody death, and general use of force legal parameters. These interviews have been well received and I have never been misquoted. It can be said that in at least two interviews that the reporter was "fishing" and trying to get me off topic. Homework is vital in these interviews and you must maintain a strong commitment to "staying on topic and on point."

It is important to note that regardless of the repartee that may exist between the PIO and reporter, there is never anything such as an "off the record" comment or "just between you and me" opinion.

"I hope people will understand that police operations are very complicated, very difficult, sometimes they're very hard to understand. Obviously when a member of the community is hurt it is understandable that people become emotional about that and, the most important message is that we need to refrain from a rush to judgment. That things may not always be as they appear and we want people to give the officers, these are public servants – good men and women doing a very difficult job and the least that we can do is provide them the benefit of the doubt while the investigations are going on."

Dr. Alexis Artwohl, Lane County I.D.F.I.T.
(Interagency Deadly Force Investigation Team) video,
Lane County, Oregon District Attorney's Office

CHAPTER 8

USE OF FORCE INVESTIGATION REPORT

Everyone in the process – the officer, supervisors, agency, city, suspect and public benefit from a good use of force investigation...*everyone.* That said, the investigative report is the evidence that such a good, professional and proper investigation was completed and how. Additionally, like the officer's use of force report it will serve as the primary means by which the agency will defend itself in court whether criminal (local, state or federal) as well as civil (state or federal).

The report is the record of what the officer's did in their words, what witnesses were available and what they saw, the suspect's own words via a tape recorded statement as well as evidence reports and images (either still shot photos or video). This investigation report comprises part of a *package* which contains all essential information in one easily referred to file.

The report should start as all reports with:

- Date of Incident   Time of Incident   Report #
- Subject/Person Arrested Name
- Case Number
- Charges
- Location of Incident
- Arresting Officers
- Officers Involved in Force

The first page of the Supervisor's Assault on Officer/Use of Force/Resisting Arrest Report of Investigation should contain a checkbox section at the top listing:

Type of Incident:

- ☐ Assault on an Officer
- ☐ Resisting Arrest
- ☐ Use of Force – Injury
- ☐ Use of Force – No Injury

This is to simplify record keeping and statistical analysis.

The next checkbox section is:

Contents:

Officer(s) Injured	Y ☐ N ☐	Photos	Y ☐ N ☐
Subject Injured	Y ☐ N ☐	Use of Force Report	Y ☐ N ☐
Taped Statements	Y ☐ N ☐	Incident Report	Y ☐ N ☐
Witness(es)	Y ☐ N ☐	Computer Aided	
		Dispatch Call Printout	Y ☐ N ☐
Arrested	Y ☐ N ☐	Evidence Report(s)	Y ☐ N ☐
Patrol Car Video	Y ☐ N ☐	Other Video	Y ☐ N ☐

Witness information such as: Name, DOB, Address and Phone, should be included. Date of Birth is included to help identify witnesses later if they move.

Witness and suspect statements should include a synopsis of the taped interview. Is it necessary to completely recount the entire interview? Not in my opinion on a standard use of force with no injury. A taped record exists which serves as the actual record of the statement. A brief synopsis of the statements will suffice to hit the high points of what witnesses saw and heard.

The two most important parts of the report are:

- Your (the investigator) actions taken, and
- Your conclusions based on the facts in evidence

The actions taken section will serve as the permanent record to stave off accusations of supervisor nonfeasance or malfeasance and used by you to document the thoroughness and professionalism of your investigation. This report will serve as the record to prevent accusations and civil actions of "Failure to Supervise" so common in today's litigious society.

Quite honestly, if your people did the right thing they and you need to properly document it.

This is in keeping with the first three rules of leadership: take care of the troops, take care of the troops, and take care of the troops.

This is not to say that your job is *not* to hold your officers accountable for their actions reference their use of force. That's absolutely the purpose of your investigation. By completing a professional and thorough investigation you support those officers in the right and weed out and initiate discipline, up to and including termination, for those officers who are wrong.

It is nonsensical to say that weeding out police officers who use excessive force, are abusive or "bad apples" does not also serve the other members of service. As a former member of a highly active street narcotics unit I can state that I told my coworkers to be on the "up and up". I told all of them, "I'm not going to prison for none of you." It may not have been grammatically correct but we were highly trained *and experienced* in matters of search and seizure as well as use of force. We knew the law, rules, regulations as well as policies and procedures. Many of the bad actors that we encountered on a regular basis acted or resisted to the point where some sort of force was necessary but we were competent in our skills and savvy in our tactics which leant itself to effective police actions. At times it may have looked brutal but *the act of employing force whether through personal weapons; chemical, electronic or other is a basic and thereby crude or brutal human action.* However, that does not make it illegal or unreasonable.

Other areas that will benefit from your investigation are training needs – sustainment and improvement. If the training your agency provides is working, then those programs and skills will need to be sustained over time. If tactical areas such as department training on vehicle stops, tactical communication, dealing with the mentally ill, etcetera are indicated this could result in a confidential report (other than the use of force investigation report) recommending new or additional training.

Conclusions:

For those agencies which subscribe to an "objectively reasonable" standard in policy there may be two possible conclusions:

1. Within the Law & Within Policy
2. Outside the Law & a Violation of Policy

If your policy is stricter than the law and the "objective reasonableness" standard there are three conclusions that may arise:

1. Within the Law & Within Policy
2. Within the Law but a Violation of Policy *Legal but subject to department discipline
3. Outside the Law & a Violation of Policy

When examining a use of force keep in mind that there will oftentimes be things the officer did wrong or could have done better. To quote Hall and Patrick from *In Defense of Self and Others* (Caroline Academic Press; 2005), "The court in **Plakas v. Drinski** declined to review the officer's actions preceding the deadly confrontation to determine if the actions were proper. The court expressed the view that such review would "nearly always reveal that something different could have been done if the officer knew the future before it occurred. The court then addressed the suggestion that the officer's actions preceding the seizure "caused" the problem.

> "Other than random attacks, all such cases begin with the decision of a police officer to do something, to help, to arrest, to inquire. If the officer had decided to do nothing then no force would have been used. In this sense the police always causes the trouble. But it is trouble which the police officer is sworn to cause, which society pays him to cause and which, if kept within constitutional limits society praises the officer for causing."

Once your use of force package is complete, make as many copies as your policy indicates and one for yourself (never trust the official records system of your agency), sign your name and submit the packages up the chain-of-command.

Shift Commander:

Actually read the package. It is amazing how many reports or packages are sent up the chain without actually being read.

🗁 CASE STUDIES (GOOD):

"The fact that the suspect was tased by multiple officers and also administered knee strikes, punches, and kicks is indicative of the tunnel vision the officers described experiencing. Most of the officers expressed to me at the scene that due to tunnel vision they weren't even aware what other officers were doing to subdue the suspect."

"This audio and visual exclusion explains some of the minor disparities in the use of force reports. An example of this is Ofcr. Jones recalled the suspect had his left hand under his torso, but Ofcr. Smith stated the suspect's hands were over his head. Another factor contributing to the disparities is the point during the encounter that each officer became involved, and the angle at which they approached…"

🗁 CASE STUDIES (IN NEED):

"I counseled Ofc. Z about delivering any kind of blow to the head because of the potential for injury. I explained the head is a target reserved for deadly force…"

"Officers followed the guidelines concerning the authorization, implementation, investigation and documentation of the use of force by officers of the Police Dept., set forth in Procedure. The officers were also found to have not violated the Rules of the Police Department."

Officer's report:

"Officers had to forcefully put the suspect's hands behind his back until he could be handcuffed

Supervisor's report:

"immediately grabbed him by the arms and took him to the ground. I observed 6 - 7 unknown officers use their body weight to hold him down..."

The worst report of investigation in a use of force case is — no report whatsoever.

What then is the purpose of the investigative report in a use of force incident?

1. Document the investigator's actions
2. Record audiotape interviews of witnesses and suspects in a written form
3. Make a conclusion on the reasonableness of the use of force
4. Create a paper trail that can be introduced as evidence and used to prepare for any and all civil litigation
5. Document violations of policy and procedure in the use of force to be used for disciplinary reasons

The investigator must list their actions upon receipt of the call forward. I don't believe that it is necessary to totally recount and reprint the officer's use of force report (although with copy & paste it is simple enough). It is important that those audio-taped witness and suspect statements be reviewed as to their highlights. In active agencies forcing supervisors to recount every word in a taped statement is too time intensive and forces the supervisor/investigator to spend too many hours in the office typing. That said, little to no information recorded by the supervisor/investigator is of little to no use to anyone.

To review a use of force investigation is not a "tactical critique" in which you list every tactical faux pas that an officer committed. It is entirely possible that the officer did: *not wait for back-up, approached a car too soon or improperly, was rude to the suspect, did use profanity, did not use cover well, did not Taser when they should have, did give; not enough, too many, not loud enough – verbal commands, was ineffective in their force application, etc.* It is possible that the officer by their poor but lawful tactics placed themselves in the position that force had to be implemented. What's your point? It's also possible that officers could look the other way or not do anything during their tour of duty. Do we punish aggressive and proactive officers who may have made mistakes? While on the other hand, do we reward those officers who do little to nothing?

Police officers are human and will make mistakes the question I keep repeating is, "Was the force used objectively reasonable at the moment the officer used it, based on the totality of the circumstances?" If the force used was within that range of reasonableness then it is in fact lawful (and shame on agencies that don't allow their officers to use force within the law. It's hard enough out there).

Once again I believe these tactical critiques are better served in another format, perhaps a "Dutch Uncle" conversation than within a use of force investigative report.

THE PARAMETERS OF USE OF FORCE

It is tough for the supervisor/investigator to make a decision that an "awful but lawful" use of force incident (as Mike Brave calls them) was objectively reasonable. But ultimately the question comes down to:

- Did the officer have authority to act?
- Was the incident within his jurisdiction?
- Did the officer have a lawful objective for taking action?
- Were and and to what level were the circumstances:
  - Tense
  - Uncertain
  - Rapidly Evolving

- Did the suspect pose an immediate threat to the officer(s) or others? How so?
- Was the suspect actively resisting arrest? How so?
- Was the suspect attempting to evade arrest by flight? How so?
- What was the officer's use of force?
- What was the suspect's reaction to that force?
- What was the totality of the circumstances including: environment, location, lighting, response of the suspect to verbal commands, closeness of a weapon, injury or exhaustion, number of suspects, prior violence by the suspect on that call, prior knowledge of arrest activity including resisting arrest or violence, how effective the force application was, size, gender, fighting skills, and more?
- Was the use of force within the range of objective reasonableness based on the totality of the circumstances?

THE EBB AND FLOW OF FORCE APPLICATION

Police defense attorney Randy Means has described the use of force as a river with an officer operating anywhere within its banks but not being able to run aground (exceed the limits of the law). Other instructors in use of force have used a similar analogy like a wave on an oscilloscope. In this way we have an action or threatened action by the suspect and an attempt to control made by the officer. The suspect complies, continues their resistance or escalates their aggression. The officer reads this reaction by the suspect and dials back their use of force based on their perceptions, repeats an attempted control procedure, or escalates in their use of force. It is the suspect and his or her original actions and responses to force applications that drive the encounter.

What you see in a use of force is an application by an officer or officers at control and an assessment of its effectiveness. For instance, a police officer sprays a suspect with pepper spray at a distance of nine feet after the suspect threatens the officer and blades himself in a fighting stance with fists raised. The officer perceives the response by the suspect as either submission, attempts at escape, continued resistance or perhaps escalated acts of violence. In our OC spraying scenario the suspect could:

a. Grab his face and bend over screaming offering no further resistance,

b. Turn and attempt to run away,

c. Continue with his fighting stance, fist clenching and verbal threats against an officer,

d. Rush the officer swinging his fists trying to hit the officer and,

e. A combination of any and all of the above.

The officer must read the suspect's response, and within his own Sympathetic Nervous System response (fight or flight), respond based on the totality of the circumstances including and not limited to: perceptions of time, distance, environment (location), presence of other suspects, lighting, sex, size, injury, exhaustion and make a decision on what action to take. We are reminded that the court in Graham acknowledged that officers are often forced to make decisions in circumstances that are tense, uncertain and rapidly evolving.

In our scenario we'll say that the suspect does (D). He rushes toward the officer swinging wildly trying to hit the officer.

The officer's response can be from a range of options. He can continue spraying the OC spray. He can drop it and use his baton, Taser, empty-hand control via punches, kicks, knees or forearms. If his radio is in his hand he may even strike out in self-defense and inadvertently impact the suspect in the head with the portable radio. There is a large leeway to what the officer can do. Remember former FBI-SAC John Hall's statement, "The case law dealing with the use of force by law enforcement is so deferential to the officers that when they learn of it they are shocked."

So where are the rocks and shoals that indicate the parameters of lawful use of force in Randy Means' analogy? It is my opinion that if the suspect submits then the officer's use of force needs to "ratchet back." For instance the officer may not go up and begin punching the suspect in the face as he covers his head and submits, offering no further signs of aggression or resistance. Further an officer may not go up to the pepper sprayed suspect who has his head down and begin hitting him with a tactical baton as the suspect falls to the ground cowering.

Could our primary or another officer take the suspect to the ground forcefully? Yes. Could they tackle the suspect after pepper spraying him? I believe they could. Could the officer draw his baton and strike the standing suspect in the thigh after he's been sprayed with OC but refuses to get on the ground? Could an officer strike an extremely violent suspect in the head with his baton? I believe under some totality of circumstances that would be a reasonable use of force.

The timeline concept of use of force was related to me by Ken Johnson (Lt., Phoenix PD, ret.). Using this model the suspect's actions are plotted against the officer's actions. For instance, we may see the following actions when reviewing officer use of force narratives and witness statements:

Officers responded to fight call or otherwise came into contact with the suspect. Suspect was violently fighting with another suspect.

Officer Actions	Suspect Responses
Officers arrived on scene in uniform	Continued fighting
Officers gave verbal orders to stop	Suspect continued fighting
Officers gave additional warnings	Suspect continued fighting
Officer draws OC spray and gives warning	Suspect continued fighting
Officer sprays suspect with OC spray	Suspect continued fighting
Officer draws baton and gives warning	Suspect continued fighting
Officer strikes with baton	Suspect continued fighting
Officer strikes with baton repeatedly	Suspect continued fighting
Officer and partner knee strike suspect	Suspect is incapacitated
Officer handcuffs suspect	Suspect compliant

Using the timeline method we are able to illustrate that in this case the suspect had eight opportunities to comply (cooperate or surrender) when the police arrived but chose to continue fighting.

The timeline compares acts by officers to control suspects with the suspect's responses.

MULTIPLE OFFICER USE OF FORCE INCIDENTS

Can multiple officers use *collectively* the same force application that a single officer uses *individually?* I'll better explain the question. Can multiple officers engage in the same amount of force on one suspect together? Can two officers strike a suspect with their batons or can only one officer? This is not so easily answered when you consider perceptual narrowing such as tunnel vision and inattentional blindness. It is entirely possible that two or more officers trying to control the same suspect will have no knowledge of what their partner(s) was doing at the same time. During a fight or flight (SNS) response, or if they were so intent on attempting to control a suspect that they are "blind" as to what others were doing, may result in two or more officers using the same control technique.

Once again the "doesn't look good on video" incident of multiple officers using batons to attempt to subdue an offender doesn't mean the force applications are excessive.

When multiple officers are involved use the following method to keep track of their use of force application:

	Name			
Technique or Tool	Smith	Jones	Doe	Brown
Pressure Point	X			
Grabbing, Holding and Wrestling		X		X
Empty Hand Strikes or Kicks				X
OC Spray	X			
Taser			X	
Baton Strike				X

Columns can be added to indicate the suspect's response to the force application. In this way we see that although four officers used multiple applications of force, the OC spray was ineffective in forcing compliance and one of the Taser probes missed resulting in an incomplete circuit with no felt effect by the suspect. The narrative would document that it was the four baton strikes by Officer Brown which finally stopped the suspect and established control though the suspect was forcefully handcuffed by Jones and Doe, no further blows were delivered or applications of additional remote control (OC or Taser) were implemented.

IN-CUSTODY DEATH

★I am not a doctor and don't even play one on TV. Therefore my approach to this issue will be from a law enforcement perspective of one who has researched and taught this subject in basic and in-service training as well as consulted with detectives, medical examiners and coroners in cases of in-custody death investigations. Further, I have been on scene when a suspect taken into custody became unresponsive only to die in the hospital later. Nothing in the following section suggests medical recommendations or diagnosis.

I would strongly suggest the books *Sudden Deaths in Custody* by Darrell L. Ross, PhD and Theodore Chan, MD (Humana Press, 2006) and *Excited Delirium Syndrome* by Theresa Di Maio and Vincent Di Maio (CRC Press, 2006).

From the *Sudden Deaths in Custody* book I'll quote Darrell Ross, PhD:

"If an agency incurs a sudden in-custody death, members of that department should be prepared to respond to a myriad of questions and perform an investigation into the incident. Questions can range from what caused the death, whether the officers used excessive force and contributed to the death, to who ultimately should be held responsible for the death. These are not easily answered questions as sudden in-custody deaths can contain enumerable variables. Therefore, a thorough incident investigation conducted by police personnel is highly recommended."

Dr. Ross even goes on to list ten recommendations for an in-custody death investigations policy. Once again, the Ross and Chan book is worth the cost to purchase.

📁 CASE STUDY:

Officer John was off-duty on his way home from working an "extra" or off-duty job providing security for a local mall. On the State Highway in traffic ahead of him a suspect intentionally ran his vehicle into other cars causing a large traffic accident. The suspect then exited his car and began running through traffic and jumping on the hoods and roofs of the stopped motor vehicles. Officer John, in uniform, with assistance from an off-duty paramedic stops and controls the suspect. Officer John uses pressure point applications to the Mandibular Angle (pressure point above the "R" angle of the jaw and below the ear) in an attempt to handcuff the suspect. After being controlled the suspect stops breathing and dies.

The county medical examiner rules the case a homicide (death at the hands of another) when he found lateral striations in the suspect's carotid arteries in autopsy. Toxicology screens on the suspect's blood found LSD and sinus meds in his system.

I became involved in this case at the request of the Homicide Investigator when it appeared as if the medical examiner was going to rule that Officer John had choked the suspect causing his death. I met with the county prosecutor persuading her to look into the possibility of ED (Excited Delirium). The prosecutor was reluctant to consider ED as cause of death because it was known more for connection with Cocaine related death (Cocaine Psychosis). I supplied her with research material from my friend Dr. Darrell Ross, PhD who was one of the leading researchers into this phenomenon.

Further, I had received some training on in-custody death from a cardiologist at a law enforcement conference. I contacted this heart specialist who had been a combat surgeon in Vietnam. He told me that he had seen these "lateral striations or microscopic tears" in the carotid arteries of perfectly healthy 18 year old individuals in the war. He even told me that if I had wrestled or played football in school that I too probably had these tears as well.

I introduced the cardiologist to the medical examiner and just asked him to consider ED as a cause of death as well.

Although the medical examiner ruled that these carotid tears were a secondary cause of death, he ruled that the primary cause was cardiac arrest related to the LSD and sinus medication. The officer was not charged with the death.

Over the years I have been involved in approximately eight or more in-custody death investigations, on scene during one incident, as well as training officers in subject control tactics based on the latest research. I have met with, attended training from, read material by or corresponded with some of the best and brightest in this field. I'll attempt to provide a brief history as well as suggest some protocols in dealing with suspects experiencing ED and deaths in police custody by manic individuals.

IN-CUSTODY DEATH HISTORY
THE CHOKE HOLD:

I started my police career in 1980 when I began working security part-time while attending university. As part of my security work I attended a private security officer training academy which was run by members of an area police department. This 120 hour course included use of force training in both non-deadly (suspect control) and deadly force (revolver training). The use of non-deadly force was taught by a former LE officer who was (and still is) quite a legend in the martial arts. One of the techniques taught in 1980 was "tiger's mouth to the throat" or to put it another way, grabbing around a suspect's Trachea and squeezing. This was a standard for many, many years in law enforcement. The old adage was, "if they can't breathe, they can't fight." Neck restraints or "chokes" were commonly taught to police back in the day. Many of these "choke holds" had their basis in martial arts. As a matter of fact, if you attended a Judo or Jiu-Jitsu tournament this weekend or watched a UFC® (Ultimate Fighter Championship) on pay-for-view you will probably see someone give up because they can't breathe or a competitor rendered unconscious by reduced blood flow to the brain.

As used in martial arts there are two types of neck restraint – respiratory and vascular. The respiratory is the common "choke hold" and the most common of these is the bar arm choke. The practitioner encircles his opponent's neck with his arm and places the forearm against the front of the throat usually grabbing his hand with the opposite hand and squeezing backward onto the throat. In martial arts competitions the person submits by "tapping out" or is rendered unconscious through their inability to breathe.

A vascular neck restraint has also been called a "sleeper hold" and is typified by centering the subject's throat in the crook of the arm thereby protecting the Larynx and Trachea. Pressure is applied to the sides of the neck by the bicep and forearm. Once again, in competition a person can submit by "tapping out" or be rendered unconscious by reduced blood flow through the carotid arteries to the brain.

Master Instructor and now retired lawman Jim Lindell (Kansas City, MO) developed the LVNR® - Lateral Vascular Neck Restraint many years ago and it was a mainstay of many police departments. *It is important to note that the LVNR had an impressive safety record of use on the street and is an excellent form of control. This training is still available through Lindell's National Law Enforcement Training Center (NLETC).

In the 1980's researchers began looking into suspect's deaths involving the use of choke holds. In truth, many of the deaths were bar arm or respiratory restraint administered by untrained officers. Vascular restraints such as the NLETC – LVNR or the Shoulder Pin from PPCT – Pressure Point Control Tactics Inc. are viable techniques of non-deadly force.

Sadly because of improper training and liability issues neck restraints have been banned from many agencies for years. *A fall-out of banning neck restraints for many agencies was a spike in the use of punches and other blows as well as an increase in the use of the police baton. In my opinion, this resulted in more suspect injuries not less since a void was left between striking a suspect and hitting them with a baton.

POSITIONAL ASPHYXIA

In the late 1980's there were incidents of deaths in custody of subjects who had been "hogtied" or handcuffed behind their backs with their ankles either shackled with leg irons and then hooked to the handcuffs and placed in the prone or face down position. Also, "hobbles" have been used (which are essentially braided cord with snap links which are wrapped around a resisting suspect's ankles and then snapped to the handcuffs.)

In the late 1980's researchers began to study deaths of subjects in the prone hogtie position. Usually after a violent resisting arrest incident, where the suspect was taken down by multiple officers. The suspect's was positioned facedown with his arms handcuffed behind his back, shackles or hobble applied to his ankles and then attached to the handcuffs via another set of cuffs or the hobble. After a period of time the suspect suddenly ceased all activity. Paramedics were called with the subject having died in custody or at the emergency room soon after arrival.

Dr. Donald Reay was one of the leading proponents of the theory of Positional Asphyxia. From Dr. Reay's 1988 published study *Effects of Positional Restraint on Oxygen Saturation and Heart Rate Following Exercise* (The American Journal of Forensic Medicine and Pathology (1988, Raven Press, Ltd.) we read:

"This report assesses the effects on peripheral oxygen saturation and heart rate that positional restraint induces when a person is prone, handcuffed, and "hog-tied.""

"This study found positional restraint to have measurable physiological effects. While the relevance to the study of sudden and unexpected death remains unclear, positional restraint and its effects should be considered when investigating deaths in persons who were handcuffed in the prone position."

Based on a number of these types of incidents in the San Diego area, a task force was formed in 1992. Departments nationwide were surveyed. The task force published a paper which was widely distributed in law enforcement. The trend of attributing death of combative or deranged subjects who died in these types of situations while in police custody to positional asphyxia had begun. A number of agencies were sued successfully in civil actions using this research.

However, another San Diego in-custody death in 1994 preciptated a civil case with Dr. Tom Neuman and Dr. Ted Chan being consulted by the county and sheriff's agency defendants. The plaintiffs alleged that the subject's death was due to the police placing him in the prone position handcuffed behind his back after a violent resisting arrest encounter. Neuman and Chan revisited Dr. Reay's research and could not replicate the results. The Neuman and Chan results were published in the *Annals of*

Emergency Medicine in 1997 *Restraint Position and Positional Asphyxia* (Chan TC, Vilke GM, Neuman T, Clausen JL; November 1997; Volume 30), "By itself, the restraint position was not associated with any clinically relevant changes in respiratory or ventilatory function in our study population of healthy individuals with preserved ventilatory reflexes and normal pulmonary physiology. There is no evidence to suggest that hypoventilatory respiratory failure or asphyxiation occurs as a direct result of body restraint position in healthy, awake, nonintoxicated individuals with normal cardiopulmonary function at baseline."

In the 1998 Court case Dr. Reay stated under oath, "the Chan study refuted some of my earlier work that I had done, it showed that the hogtie position does not cause physiological disturbance sufficient to account for death." Further from the court transcripts (relayed to me by Dr. Darrell Ross, Dr. Reay said, "I acknowledge that my earlier work in analyzing oxygen saturation levels with arterial blood supply was in error and my fundamental hypothesis that hogtying precipitates asphyxiation because of the decrease in oxygen saturation levels were refuted by the Neuman study – yes," and "I no longer adhere to the hogtie prone position precipitating asphyxiation (based on Neuman's work)."

(Email correspondence from Dr. Darrell Ross, 29 May 2006)

From that case decision, "After Dr. Reay's retraction, little evidence is left that suggests that the hogtie restraint can cause asphyxia. All of the scientists who have sanctioned the concept of positional asphyxia have relied to some degree on Dr. Reay's work. The UCSD study has proven Reay's work to be faulty, which impugns the scientific articles that followed it. Like a house of cards, the evidence for positional asphyxia has fallen completely. In light of the UCSD study, the hogtie restraint in and of itself does not constitute excessive force – when a violent individual has resisted less severe restraint techniques, applying a physiological neutral restraint that will immobilize him is not excessive force."

(Price v. County of San Diego; Jan. 8, 1998;
990 F.Supp. 1230 (S.D. Cal.)

Although Dr. Chan has pointed out that PA (Positional Asphyxia) as perpetuated in the law enforcement field does not exist, the theorists continued stating that it was PA combined with OC spray that was killing suspects in police custody or was "compressional asphyxia" (the weight of officers on the suspects back).

Dr. Chan has studied both the effects of OC and the hogtie position as well as compressional asphyxia and determined the same conclusions as with positional asphyxia alone.

Published in *National Institute of Justice Research in Brief* (December 2001) by Theodore Chan, Gary Vilke, Jack Clausen, Richard Clark, Paul Schmidt, Thomas Snowden, and Tom Neuman is this brief *Pepper Spray's Effects on a Suspect's Ability to Breathe*. From that brief:

"Despite the success of OC spray, there is growing concern about its safety, particularly when exposure is combined with positional restraint. A number of arrestees exposed to OC, which induces coughing, gagging, and shortness of breath, have died in custody – thus prompting the allegation that OC inhalation places individuals at risk for potentially fatal respiratory compromise."

"Law enforcement implications. Study findings support the contention that OC spray inhalation, even when combined with positional restraint, poses no significant risk to subjects in terms of respiratory and pulmonary function."

"On the issue of in-custody deaths, this study indicates that OC inhalation and exposure do not cause significant respiratory injury and should not lead to an increased risk of respiratory compromise, arrest, or death – thus lending credence to the large retrospective field studies that have found little evidence that OC causes significant respiratory injury."

From *Does Weight Force During Physical Restraint Cause Respiratory Compromise?* (Gary M. Vilke, Betty Michalewicz, Fred Kolkhorst, Tom Neuman and Theodore Chan; Academic Emergency Medicine; 2005; Volume 12, Number 5), "**Background**: Violent patients often require physical restraint by emergency department (ED), out-of-hospital, and law enforcement personnel. Concern has been raised that weight force, commonly applied during the restraining process, can compromise respiratory function, placing individuals at risk for asphyxiation. **Conclusions:** Significant weight force in the prone position decreases MVV (maximal voluntary ventilation); however, we did not detect decreases below known clinical thresholds for abnormal pulmonary function."

"Based on these findings, factors other than body positioning appear to be more important determinants for sudden unexpected deaths in individuals in the hogtie custody restraint position. Illicit drug use (including sympathomimetic, hallucinogenic, and psychomotor stimulant drugs), physiologic stress, hyperactivity, hyperthermia, catechol hyperstimulation, and trauma from struggle may be more important factors in the deaths of these individuals."

> *Reexamination of Custody Restraint Position and Positional Asphyxia*
> · (Chan, Theodore C. MD, Vilke, Gary M., MD, Neuman, Tom MD; The American Journal of Forensic Medicine and Pathology; September, 1998)

TASER®

*Let me state that I am not currently a Taser instructor, although I did go through a Taser Instructor certification course several years ago. For more precise information about the Taser I would suggest you attend a certified training program.

🗁 CASE STUDY:

Two incidents of in-custody death were set to be ruled on by the Medical Examiner. Both incidents involved subjects under the influence of drugs and experiencing symptoms of Excited Delirium. I was asked to contact the Medical Examiner and speak to her about the cases and possibly reviewing the latest research on ED with her as well as connecting her to one of the best researchers on in-custody death in the United States. My focus was not to defend Taser International (something that they can more ably do…) but rather to focus on ED as the possible potential cause of death in both cases.

I remember driving down the street being called by the local prosecutor's office with an assistant prosecutor asking me if I could get the M.E. to withhold releasing a cause of death until she had spoken to the experts I knew. I laughed at the thought of a Patrolman being asked to do this...

The M.E. refused to acknowledge ED as a cause of death and instead attributed it to the electrical shock of the Taser.

Taser International sued the M.E.'s office in State Court. The M.E. was unable to defend her ruling as the science of the use of the Taser and its medical impact was clearly against her. The Judge ordered that Taser be removed from the M.E.'s report as the cause of death and show that the death was due to "undetermined" causes.

I won't cover the scientific and other research that Taser International has put into their products. Suffice to say that the Taser remains an excellent tool for controlling mentally ill subjects as well as criminal suspects who are resisting arrest or threatening assault against law enforcement officers.

Although mental illness advocacy groups will not come right out and endorse the use of the Taser, it has been proven to reduce injury to mentally ill subjects that are out of control versus standard police use of force methodologies – OC spray, striking and baton for instance.

Even in subject's experiencing Excited Delirium, the Taser is still the recommended method for quick control versus prolonged struggles with an EDP – Emotionally Disturbed Person. The Taser is the control tool of choice for the majority of officers who are specially trained to deal with mentally ill persons in crisis.

★Michael Brave, Esq. Taser's lead counsel is a treasure trove of information not only about the Taser but also about the law. If you ever have the opportunity to attend a course by Mr. Brave, I strongly recommend it. According to Michael Brave (ILEETA Presentation, April 2010) as of that date there had been:

- over 2,177,000 Taser Electronic Control Device applications to humans (1,070,785 field use applications and 1,107,033 training/voluntary applications)

- over 499,000 Taser ECD's in use in more than 40 countries worldwide.

With all those Tasers in use and all those recorded applications to humans, it is safe to say that Taser has an amazing safety record.

"Almost every use of force, however minute, poses some risk of death."

> Garrett v. Athens-Clarke County,
> 378 F.3d 1274, n.12 (11th Cir. 2004).

EXCITED DELIRIUM

🗁 CASE STUDY:

A patrol officer and sergeant in a small Midwestern town respond to 911 calls of a shirtless male terrorizing a neighborhood by running around smashing porch windows. When the patrol officer turns onto the street where the calls are coming from, he sees a naked man bleeding from a neck wound running toward him. The officer's first thoughts are the man is a crime victim running from a suspect. That is until, the subject runs and jumps onto the patrol car hood over the roof and off the trunk. The sergeant who is directly behind the officer sees the male who now is now at her driver's door window banging on it, with a knife in his hand. The window explodes inward as the sergeant is able to get her service pistol out and fires two rounds at the suspect. The suspect dies from his wounds.

In scenes repeated too frequently throughout the country this subject, who was under the influence of PCP and Psilocybin mushrooms, was experiencing Excited Delirium (ED).

Far from a new experience, ED also known as Bell's Mania was first attributed as a cause of death by Dr. Luther Bell in 1849. According to Theresa Di Maio and Vincent Di Maio in their book *Excited Delirium Syndrome: Cause of Death and Prevention* (CRC Press; 2006), "Dr. Bell thought he was describing a new disease, a fatal form of delirium in the mentally ill. Typically, patients presented with fever, a rapid pulse, a lack of appetite and sleep. They were agitated and anxious, with increasing confusion that appeared suddenly. Any attempt to approach the patient resulted in a violent struggle. Typically, the patient continued to deteriorate over a course of weeks before dying."

According to Dr. Charles Wetli in *Sudden Deaths in Custody* (Chapter 7; Humana Press; 2006):

Common Presenting Features of Excited Delirium Syndrome

- Acute psychotic behavior
- Violent agitation
- Altered mental status and delirium
- Bizarre behaviors (e.g. jumping through windows)
- Profuse sweating
- Incoherent speech (screaming and shouting)
- Extraordinary strength and endurance
- Lack of response to painful stimuli
- Extreme exertion and hyperactivity
- Hyperthermia

Dr. Wetli goes on to state, "It has been estimated that approximately 10% of cases of excited delirium result in fatality.

According to Dr. Darrel Ross, Cocaine, Methamphetamine, Cocaine and alcohol, Marijuana, Benzoylecogine, Lithium, LSD and several more drugs have been linked to in-custody deaths of an arrestee.

Dr. Ross states in Chapter 9 of *Sudden Deaths in Custody* (Humana Press; 2006), "Although sudden in-custody death is rare in occurrence, the incident comprises a myriad of potential contributing factors that can make determining a cause of death problematic. Numerous questions of what contributed to the sudden death arise."

If at all possible core body temperature should be taken at the scene of death or as quickly as possible by the coroner investigators or ER doctors. Elevated core temperatures are frequently recorded. The Di Maio's state in their book, "Hyperthermia is not uncommon in cases of excited delirium syndrome. The exact incidence is unknown because body temperature is often not taken if death is rapid."

In one case I am aware of body temperature was not taken until four hours after death and was still 104 degrees Fahrenheit.

📁 CASE STUDY:

A subject under the influence of Crack Cocaine is found running through the streets after calls for police assistance by neighbors. He is brought under control and transported to the local Emergency Room where he recovers.

One month later the same suspect once again under the influence of Cocaine in the same neighborhood on a similar call is taken into custody where he soon dies.

Same subject, same drug, same Excited Delirium Syndrome behavior. One incident he lives the other he dies…

What we are forced to deal with in confronting and controlling a subject under the influence of Excited Delirium is as Canadian police ED researcher Chris Lawrence has said, "someone who is very hard to control but very fragile." This dichotomy is what officers face in the street. Their use of force in controlling an ED subject must be objectively reasonable in light of the totality of the circumstances.

To develop totality of the circumstances it might be beneficial as Drs. James Luke and Donald Reay state in *The Perils of Investigating and Certifying Deaths in Police Custody* (The American Journal of Forensic Medicine and Pathology (Raven Press, 13(2); 1992) to develop:

> "A step-by-step, freeze-frame, specific sequential scenario of the confrontation(s) between law enforcement and the person being detained must be developed. For obvious reasons, this should be accomplished as soon after the event is practical, with participants sequestered for questioning. It is essential that all witnesses and participants understand the importance of developing reliable information – information that, because it emanates independently from different sources, can be shown to be reproducible and to represent what is likely to have happened."

For years Excited Delirium was not a recognized condition or disease. Yes, Bell's Mania was accepted as was Acute Exhaustive Mania but ED remained unaccepted. According to Dr. Charles Wetli in his chapter in *Sudden Deaths in Custody* the medical community has been slow to accept ED: "Despite growing recognition of the hallmarks of excited delirium syndrome, some question the actual existence of this clinical entity. Although the National Association of Medical Examiners has recognized this syndrome for more than a decade, the American Medical Association does not recognize this diagnosis as a medical or psychiatric condition."

In September, 2009 a taskforce from the American College of Emergency Physicians® (ACEP) published a report titled *White Paper Report on Excited Delirium Syndrome.* From that report:

> "In modern times, a law enforcement officer (LEO) is often present with a person suffering from ExDS because the situation at hand has degenerated to such a degree that someone has deemed it necessary to contact a person of authority to deal with it. LEOs are in the difficult and sometimes impossible position of having to recognize this as a medical emergency, attempting to control an irrational and physically resistive person, and minding the safety of all involved."

> "Given the irrational and potentially violent, dangerous, and lethal behavior of an ExDS subject, any LEO interaction with a person in this situation risks significant injury or death to either the LEO or the ExDS subject who has a potentially lethal medical syndrome. This already challenging situation has the potential for intense public scrutiny coupled with the expectation of a perfect outcome. Anything less creates a situation of potential public outrage. Unfortunately, this dangerous medical situation makes perfect outcomes difficult in many circumstances."

> "ExDS subjects are known to be irrational, often violent and relatively impervious to pain. Unfortunately, almost everything taught to LEOs about control of subjects relies of a suspect to either be rational, appropriate, or to comply with

painful stimuli. Tools and tactics available to LEOs (such as pepper spray, impact batons, joint lock maneuvers, punches and kicks, and ECD's (Electronic Control Devices), especially when used for pain compliance) that are traditionally effective in controlling resisting subjects, are likely to be less effective on ExDS subjects."

"When methods such as pain compliance maneuvers or tools of force fail, the LEO is left with few options. It is not feasible for them to wait for the ExDS subject to calm down, as this may take hours in a potentially medically unstable situation fraught with scene safety concerns."

ACEP lists these "Prehospital Potential Features" (actions or conditions of those experiencing ExDS):

Pain Tolerance	100%
Tachypnea	100%
Sweating	95%
Agitation	95%
Tactile Hyperthermia	95%
Police Noncompliance	90%
Lack of Tiring	90%
Unusual Strength	90%
Inappropriately Clothed	70%
Mirror / Glass Attraction	10%

"When death occurs, it occurs suddenly, typically following physical control measures (physical, noxious chemical, or electrical), and there is no clear anatomic cause of death at autopsy. In cases in which a subject dies following the application of control measures, many or most of the following features are found:

- Male subjects, average age 36
- Destructive or bizarre behavior generating calls to police,

- Suspected or known psychostimulant drug or alcohol intoxication,
- Suspected or known psychiatric illness,
- Nudity or inappropriate clothing for the environment,
- Failure to recognize or respond to police presence at the scene (reflecting delirium),
- Erratic or violent behavior,
- Unusual physical strength and stamina,
- Ongoing struggle despite futility,
- Cardiopulmonary collapse immediately following a struggle or very shortly after quiescence,
- Inability to be resuscitated at the scene, and
- Inability for a pathologist to determine a specific organic cause of death,
- Attraction to glass or reflective surfaces (less frequent than all others per the Canadian data).

"Based upon available evidence, it is the consensus of the Task Force that ExDS is a real syndrome of uncertain etiology. It is characterized by delirium, agitation, and hyperadrenergic autonomic dysfunction, typically in the setting of acute or chronic drug abuse or serious mental illness."

🗁 CASE STUDY:

Officers respond to a residence reference a domestic fight. Call notes forwarded by dispatch via the in car computer system indicate that "a male was breaking windows, was bleeding and was lying out on the curb." EMS was reported en route. As the officers pulled up they observed a white male on his hands and knees erratically rocking back and forth on the curb. Despite his calls for help, the subject would not respond to the officer's questions. Two females were on the porch and yelled out that the subject on the curb had just broken into their house and the police should watch out because he was dangerous. Witnesses stated that the subject had ripped off his shirt and ran outside. The officers handcuff the suspect for their own safety and he attempts to bite one officer in the process. EMS arrives and begins treating the subject. When he is placed on the gurney he becomes unresponsive he is immediately transported to the local Emergency Room where he soon dies.

Later investigations will indicate that the subject had been smoking Crack Cocaine in the house when he suddenly "began acting crazy." He started throwing furniture in the house. After he was forcibly thrown out of the house by the occupants, he broke several windows before officers arrived and found him at the curb.

The Medical Examiner's Report indicates:

Cause of death: Probable cardiac arrhythmia. Due to: Cocaine delirium. II: Cocaine abuse. ACCIDENT: Adverse reaction to cocaine.

Sadly I have had several friends who were involved in similar incidents which involved resisting suspects who later died in custody. Some were ruled "Homicide" others were ruled accidental. Drugs involved have ranged from LSD, GHB, Meth, Oxy, Cocaine and a combination of these with alcohol. These use-of-force investigations can be traumatic for the officer involved and can generate much media attention.

As I indicated to start this section, I was present when a subject was taken into custody who became unresponsive only to die in the hospital later. As a member of a police tactical team we had conducted a search warrant for narcotics detectives at the suspect's apartment in a housing project in our city. The suspect fled out the back door as we executed the warrant through the front door. He was tackled and taken into custody after a short foot chase. After the warrant we were standing outside the back door, the same area as the suspect who had been handcuffed behind his back and placed on the ground face down. The suspect began complaining that he did not feel well. We were later to learn that the suspect had just got done smoking $150.00 worth of Crack Cocaine just before we executed the warrant.

He died in the hospital five days later after going into a coma. He did not recover post emergency surgery after a C.T. scan revealed acute cerebellar hemorrhage and intraventricular hemorrhage.

The Medical Examiner's report indicates cause of death as: Cardiorespiratory arrest. Due to: Brain swelling with herniation. Due to: Spontaneous intracerebellar and intraventricular hemorrhage. Due to: Hypertension, acute, due to cocaine intoxication complicated by sympathetic discharge (panic and anxiety). ACCIDENTAL: Deceased, history of cocaine use, running from police raid, sustained severe acute hypertension.

Although neither my teammates nor I were investigated in this death, this was 20 years ago and times were different. Such death in-custody events garner much more media attention and are oftentimes spurned by special interest, anti-police groups who refuse to accept the realities of ED focusing instead on the police actions.

Are all subjects (under the influence of drugs or alcohol) who have died in custody after use of force encounters with the police, experiencing excited delirium? Obviously not but it does explain many of the deaths of otherwise healthy subjects absent any obvious causes of death.

True, the police are involved in these events but it is sad that a medical group such as the American College of Emergency Physicians has stated, "When methods such as pain compliance maneuvers or tools of force fail, the LEO is left with few options. It is not feasible for them to wait for the ExDS subject to calm down, as this may take hours in a potentially medically unstable situation fraught with scene safety concerns," while at the same time, members of the criminal justice community as well as some medical examiners are ignorant of the phenomenon of excited delirium or refuse to accept it.

CHAPTER 9

CHAIN-OF-COMMAND RESPONSIBILITIES

Each use of force should be reviewed by the chain-of-command up to and including the chief of police. In most cases the patrol division of an agency will be handling most of these investigations. That will mean patrol sergeants, lieutenants, captains, majors up to the chief depending on your agency's command structure. Additionally these reports should be forwarded to: training, internal affairs, and any oversight group or person such as civilian review boards and police auditors (Note – dissemination and review by civilian oversight may have contractual implications. Union contracts should be addressed.) Certainly all of the reports included in the package are public record and accessible through public records laws in your state.

FRONT-LINE SUPERVISOR (USE OF NON-DEADLY FORCE):

The primary investigator/responding supervisor (usually a sergeant) is tasked with responding to the scene and should:

- Ensure injuries of officer(s), suspects and victims are addressed
- Debrief the officer(s) involved as to the situation and general explanation of what transpired

- Order use of force reports from ALL officers involved – whether participants or observers (this includes officers who "didn't see a thing)
- Elicit the details of what happened before, during and after the use of force. It is important that officers give more than "we took him down to the ground" or the like
- Interview witnesses and suspects (on audiotape)
- Survey the scene
- Take photos (scene, officers, suspects)
- Ensure evidence is properly identified and gathered
- Identify videotape sources (patrol car cams, stationhouse systems, jail video & surveillance cameras) and obtain copies or begin the process to obtain disks or tapes
- Take notes of activities for inclusion in the use of force investigation report
- Obtain copies of call notes if germane
- Obtain copies of dispatch tapes if germane
- Review use of force reports as delivered by involved personnel, edit and recommend changes, modifications
- Document actions
- Review officer(s) actions and determine if the use of force was objectively reasonable (within the law), within policy *or* not reasonable and/or out of policy
- Forward the package up the chain-of-command

FRONT-LINE SUPERVISOR (DEADLY FORCE):

The front-line supervisor (usually a sergeant) is tasked with responding to the scene and should:

- Ensure that the scene is safe
- If the scene is still unsafe or suspects are still unsecured, coordinate the police response
- Ensure injuries of officer(s), suspects and victims are addressed
- Ascertain if the suspect(s) are in custody
- If a suspect is not in custody, interview the officer involved to: obtain description(s), direction of travel, possible charges and officer safety information (is armed, etc.)

- Debrief officer and visually examine officer's uniform and/or weapons to determine evidence protection and value (including blood splatter, tissue evidence and possible suspect fingerprints)
- If the officer(s)' firearms have evidentiary value secure them for DB investigators but provide the officer with a replacement or initiate the process to obtain a replacement firearm for the officer
- If scene is unsafe or hostile, remove officer(s) involved from that location
- "Partner up" the involved officer(s) with another patrolman to see that they are safe
- Suggest that the involved officer(s) be careful about talking about the specifics of the incident to other patrol officers
- Obtain a union shift representative to protect the rights of the officer(s)
- Detail officers to check the impact points of errant bullet strikes by the police and by the suspect
- Locate and identify the physical crime scene(s) and evidence
- Assign officers to secure the scene via crime scene tape and protect evidence against: theft by third parties; destruction due to police, fire or medic personnel; destruction or loss due to the conditions (wind, rain, snow)
- Locate and identify witnesses
- Ensure "action taken" reports are generated for DB personnel by patrol officers on scene

*Not in order of importance

PATROL SHIFT COMMANDER OR ASSISTANT SHIFT COMMANDER (USE OF NON-DEADLY FORCE):

- Monitor the call to determine if your presence is required
- Respond if officers are injured
- Respond as needed or available
- Debrief front-line supervisor as to the nature and extent of use of force incident and package completion
- Read, review and inspect package for content and proper completion

- Recommend additional training
- Sustain or Improve training, officer(s)' & supervisor's response(s) or investigatory process
- Sign and forward

SHIFT COMMANDER OR ASSISTANT SHIFT COMMANDER (USE OF DEADLY FORCE):

- Respond to the scene and assume overall command of patrol officers and sergeants

Delegate or personally see that the following are accomplished:
- Ensure that the scene is safe
- If the scene is still unsafe or suspects are still unsecured, coordinate the police response
- Ensure injuries of officer(s), suspects and victims are addressed
- Ascertain if the suspect(s) are in custody
- If a suspect is not in custody, interview the officer involved to: obtain description(s), direction of travel, possible charges and officer safety information (armed, etc.)
- Debrief officer and visually examine officer's uniform and/or weapons to determine evidence protection and value (including blood splatter, tissue evidence and possible suspect fingerprints)
- If the officer(s)' firearms have evidentiary value, secure them for DB investigators but provide the officer with a replacement or initiate the process to obtain a replacement firearm for the officer
- If scene is unsafe or hostile, remove officer(s) involved from that location
- "Partner up" the involved officer(s) with another patrolman to see that they are safe
- Suggest that the involved officer(s) be careful about talking about the specifics of the incident to other patrol officers
- Obtain a union shift representative to protect the rights of the officer(s)
- Detail officers to check the impact points of errant bullet strikes by the police and by the suspect
- Locate and identify the physical crime scene(s) and evidence

- Assign officers to secure the scene via crime scene tape and protect evidence against: theft by third parties, destruction due to police, fire or medic personnel; destruction or loss due to the conditions (wind, rain, snow)
- Locate and identify witnesses
- Ensure "action taken" reports are generated for DB personnel by patrol officers on scene
- Generate a Commander's Report to document actions taken
- Notify Commander and Chief

INTERNAL AFFAIRS INVESTIGATION OR AGENCY INTERNAL REVIEW OF DEADLY FORCE:

It is important to note here that depending on agency size and structure detectives from Homicide or General Assignment may be the primary investigators for officer involved shootings.

With many agencies and current budget issues, the on-shift or on-call detective regardless of specialty may respond. This investigator may or may not have received advanced training on the intricacies of the use of deadly force investigation. If they have not received training (or haven't read this book) they may respond as if they are responding to "just another" shooting call or their first homicide investigation in quite a while. This can taint the investigation as well as possibly inflict damage on the officer and agency morale.

Experience in these investigations can be a good thing (twenty years experience in officer involved shooting investigations) or a bad thing (one year's experience repeated twenty times). Regardless, as we have seen, this is a specialized investigative procedure. Although the facts are gathered and supplied to the prosecutor or district attorney as in any other felonious assault or homicide investigation the *means, methods and procedures of the investigation* are different since police officers are charged by the state to use deadly force if required. They've done their duty, we owe it to them to review properly.

This can lend itself to tremendous opportunities to second guess the officer. "I don't think this was a good shoot," or "The officer could have done this or that differently."

Many of these opportunities for Monday morning quarterbacking (or 20/20 hindsight as the Supreme Court warned against in Graham v. Connor as well as Prakas v. Drinski) have been self-induced by law enforcement agencies or trainers.

Issues such as: intent, ability, opportunity, jeopardy and preclusion were put forth and touted by LE personnel to help clarify use of force decisions and to prevent tragedies from occurring. Quite the opposite has been the result with an officer's judgment clouded on when to shoot because of massive restrictions imposed by their own agency.

🗀 CASE STUDY:

Veteran federal use of force trainer John Bostain told me of a case in which he was approached by a firearms training supervisor who stated that current scientific research on officer response time to armed threats conducted by Dr. Bill Lewinski of Force Science was wrong. According to Bostain the supervisor stated he would not train his officers in the research because he believed it made them "trigger happy." He instead believed that officers out in the open without any cover would have time to respond to the drawing or movement of a suspect's gun, and be able to shoot and neutralize the threat.

Here, sadly, was a law enforcement trainer and firearms supervisor who because of his feelings of "trigger happy cops" was unwilling to provide his officers with the latest scientific research on human response time – something that has the potential to improve their safety and chance of going home. Research that, had he made them aware of or taught them, could potentially be used to defend them because it could be part of their pre-shooting "mindset" and training.

As John has stated, this is a serious example of law enforcement "cluelessness."

The first and foremost question is the legalities of the shoot. Was it an objectively reasonable use of deadly force based on the officer's reasonable perceptions to the totality of the circumstances?

Quite honestly, the investigator's or supervisor's personal versus professional opinion doesn't matter. You may feel that the officer was: angry at the suspect, unprofessional in his communication skills, tactically deficient, etcetera. That may or may not be true but the question is whether the core law enforcement transaction was lawful and whether the use of deadly or non-deadly force was within the parameters of law.

Subsequent to the criminal investigation or run at the same time is the internal investigation. The internal review is to focus on rules, regulations, policy and procedures. As stated in Chapter 4 on Agency Policy, why an agency would make a stricter policy than federal and state law is beyond me.

The internal investigation may start with an interview of the officer(s) separate from any criminal investigation. Since this interview is for an internal investigation an officer does not have the right to refuse to give a statement.

All parties involved in use of force investigation should receive specialized training in this area. Too often I've seen ill informed opinion presented as investigative conclusions to condemn an officer who did nothing wrong versus factual, scientific and use of force law informed decisions. This type of investigative result undercuts officer morale and confidence that officers on the street will be supported if they do the right thing.

Supervisor Responsibilities:

📁 CASE STUDY:

"Donny" is a highly respected and active patrol supervisor. He was standing at a photocopy machine copying an article from a magazine on search and seizure. Another supervisor of higher rank walked by and inquired what he was doing. He responded that he was copying the article on the 4th Amendment to give to his troops. The other supervisor said, "Oh, the 4th Amendment that's about guns isn't it?"

📁 CASE STUDY:

"Harry" was the commander of a highly active street level narcotics unit. The unit was at the "pointy end of the spear" when it came to street level narcotics arrests, search warrants and the like. Harry would routinely conduct impromptu classes on Search & Seizure and constitutional law to his troops. The result was no civil

suits during his tenure or allegations of improper search and seizure. No complaints of violations of any suspect's 4th Amendment rights, no evidence tossed out at suppression hearings, all of which led to an amazing conviction rate for offenders arrested by the unit.

📁 CASE STUDY:

Supervisors are tasked with reviewing an officer's use of force and conclude that the force used was excessive. Subjective elements – anger and officer's malicious intent are alleged as well as accusations of poor tactics prior to the incident. The officer is suspended. The officer's union hires an expert who looks at the administrative decision and determines that the use of force was clearly within the law. When the supervisors are tasked with their decision they remark, "The expert had access to use of force measuring tools not available to us." The expert turns to the agency policy and points out that all the tools are contained therein.

These three case studies point out the need for supervisors to constantly research, study and review use of force law and agency policy. The 4th Amendment and its role in search and seizure law are paramount. Like the in-service legal training conducted by prosecutors, district attorneys or police legal advisors on legal updates, each and every police officer must have a working knowledge of use of force. Too many agencies, in my opinion, focus on policy as the standard governing use of force. As I mentioned earlier in this manual, policy should be based on federal and state law and those legal standards incorporated into policy standards. That said, far too many supervisors have forgotten Graham v. Connor and Tennessee v. Garner which they learned in their basic academy.

That is simply not acceptable.

In order to perform their leadership role supervisors must know Federal and State standards for use of force. It is not an option.

Further, to properly "lead" their troops (remember the first three rules of leadership: take care of the troops, take care of the troops, take care of the troops!) they should continually train officers in their charge in search and seizure including use of force. The better officers know the law, the better decisions they'll make. This holds true for supervisors as well.

As a trainer I would make some overall points and suggestions for supervisors in general on use of force, as well as those dealing with an officer worth saving who is having use of force problems (increased frequency) or sustained citizen complaints:

- Go out in the field and see how your officers work. By having daily or weekly interactions you'll get an idea of their actions that need sustained or improved.
- Pull them aside and pat them on the back for their actions as well as have those "Dutch Uncle" conversations about their deficits or your concerns.
- For supervisors or agencies, document. Keep records of the incidents and contacts you've had with the officer: "Dutch Uncle" conversations, informal and formal discipline (write-ups and notices). The rule is that if it isn't on paper – it didn't happen.
- Recommend remediation in such topics as use of force law, policy & procedure, tactics, suspect control skills and firearms training.
- Publically acknowledge a good use of force or good use of force report. This lets them know you're paying attention and that if they do it right, you'll back them up.
- Consider that the problem is not the action they took on the street but rather their poor use-of-force report writing.
- Recommend reading assignments such as reading John Hall & Urey Patrick's book *In Defense of Self and Others* or other books listed in the references and suggested reading section of this manual.
- Read police periodicals and reprint topical articles about such issues as search and seizure, Miranda, use of force, Terry Stops and Terry Frisks and more. This will keep you sharp about the law as well as serve your troops.
- Recommend additional training programs. There are excellent programs on police use of force law as well as physical skill training throughout this country.
- Send the officer to *Verbal Judo*® training or similar to focus on their communications skills.

- Have their body language evaluated by an expert. There are specialists in the private sector who consult on body language.
- Partner up a good solid communicator and professional officer with someone who is in need. Mentoring is an extremely powerful tool to pass on good habits and tactics.

USE OF FORCE "TRACKING" AND FREQUENCY OF USE-OF-FORCE INCIDENTS:

I believe it is completely appropriate for agencies to "track" or document the frequency with which officers use force. Certainly frequency can be an early warning sign of an officer in need of remedial training.

What an agency and supervisors cannot do is to acknowledge that there is a problem officer and not act. An officer everyone in the agency knows who could get a room full of nuns to riot (whether through their body language since over 80% of communication is non-verbal), a condescending attitude, or poor communication skills, these officers can and do (in the vernacular of the street) "ass up" most everyone. You cannot standby, waiting until he or she finally does the one big thing that results in termination. This "ticking time-bomb" method exposes the supervision of the agency as well as the governmental body it works for to serious liability exposure.

Is arrest activity or street activity a guarantee of increased frequency of use of force? Some will say that complaints and use of force goes hand in hand with aggressive street enforcement. In my opinion it is not a guaranteed result. That does not mean that officers or units of officers who work in busy/violent districts, gang units or street drug enforcement because of the nature of their work might receive more citizen complaints or have a greater frequency of use of force. There are officers in these very same units who are just as active and do not receive complaints or higher number of use of force incidents. Attitude, demeanor, professionalism, communications and training background are important ingredients in violence control strategies on the street.

Agencies therefore have a verifiable reason to track use of force numbers and to suggest or order remedial or specialized training. To offer control strategies as well as document these attempts and the officer's acceptance, rejection, success or failure.

To paraphrase veteran LE trainer Gordon Graham, "This is not a guaranteed job for life. There is selection and there is de-selection." If an officer is intentionally abusive or brutal it is the agency's responsibility to identify and discipline him. If progressive discipline is not successful in modifying his behavior or the abuse so egregious, then termination should result. There is a difference between an officer whose actions are unintentional and one who is intentionally and knowingly abusing his authority.

This does not mean that a poor communicator or an officer with a condescending attitude cannot have a perfectly good use of force incident. Since each incident must be investigated on its own merit, increased numbers of these incidents doesn't make one (or all of them) bad.

Is there a magic number of incidents which means you're dealing with a "brutal cop?" Absolutely not, but by you and your agency paying attention – rewarding good police work and identifying and remediating poor police work – you'll show the troops that there is only one acceptable way to do the job, the right way.

If you are investigating an abusive cop or have determined that the officer in question has used excessive force then be meticulous in your investigation, paperwork and documentation. What I mean by that is to review federal and state use of force law, appropriate policies and procedures and then properly complete and document the investigation. Far too many times bad officers who should be terminated retain their jobs because of poor internal investigations. A supervisor can blame it all they want on the union or union lawyers but if a solid case is served up against an abusive cop then the chips must fall where they may. In truth the police union and its membership are better off when a bad cop is booted out because he exposes every member who works with him to risk.

We must keep in mind that it is a truism in law enforcement that supervisors may want a shift or street activity to be as boring and quiet as possible, while young, aggressive patrolmen want to make things as exciting as possible. Young, aggressive officers must be trained and mentored properly to develop an aggressive but legal use of force climate.

Leadership is the driving force on *use-of-force:* from administrators and supervisors allowing officers to use the range of force options as dictated by the courts. Leadership is staying away from overly restrictive policies, training your officers to the best of your abilities, backing them when they do the right thing and properly investigating and documenting a use of force incident.

Educate yourself about the constitutional standards, federal and state law as well as agency policy and then lead your troops.

CHAPTER 10

FINAL THOUGHTS

📁 CASE STUDY:

Officer "Smith" was a good officer. Diligent and smart he aggressively but fairly enforced the law in Gotham City. His agency however, had yielded to the notion that it could reduce its liability exposure and be more "modern" by having an extensive use of force policy which incorporated a continuum. The policy was 50 pages long and dealt with all manner of officer subject factors, force considerations, restrictions on shooting at or from moving vehicles and more. The training vendor who sold the agency administrators on the extensive policy pointed out that he had large volumes of research to support this document which exceeded the law and restricted officers. The vendor pointed out that an important selling point was that he was available for professional witness work should they ever be sued. He suggested that having officers fill out a form every time they drew their pistols from their holsters, would help protect the agency from civil litigation if and when a shooting ever happened.

Gotham P.D. never trained their officers in use of force and never trained their supervisors in use of force investigations. Two officers had been disciplined and terminated for excessive use of force only to get their jobs back in an arbitrator's hearing when experts hired by the union proved the use of force was lawful as well as within policy. The impact on officer morale was devastating. Officers had no confidence in their agency that if they used force, the bosses would competently investigate the incident. Use of force incidents on the street went down, but so did officer activity. Fewer traffic stops and suspicious person investigations and less officer initiated police work resulted in reduced felony and misdemeanor arrests. Crime wasn't down but arrests and activity were.

So when Gotham P.D. Officer Smith confronted three suspects at zero-dark-thirty in the loading zone behind a closed retail store, the stage was set for tragedy. Standing around a darkened motor vehicle with an open trunk, the suspects caused the hairs on his neck to stand on end. Smith was reluctant to draw his pistol as it might be reflected in his personal evaluations as being too aggressive and he'd have to fill out that dang form. Instead the Gotham officer approached the suspects and asked non-aggressively, "Hey, guys what's up?" In the beam of his flashlight he saw a pry bar lying nearby and the trunk of the car filled with store merchandise. "Hey guys let me see your hands," he ordered as he reached out to grab the closest suspect's arm to pivot him around. The suspect pulled his arm away. Smith thought "is that defensive resistance or active aggression?" "Can I use soft or hard empty hand control techniques?" Before he can mentally answer the question, the suspect punched Officer Smith in the mouth and knocked him to the ground. Smith yelled at the suspect, "Stop!" just prior to being kicked in the head. He attempted to draw his electronic control device but it was kicked aside as the other suspects joined in the kicking frenzy on the downed officer. Smith didn't even think to draw his own pistol prior to being rendered unconscious by a vicious blow to the head.

Once Officer Smith was unconscious one of the suspects reached down and removed his duty pistol from his holster. Standing over the prostrate and helpless officer he fired multiple rounds into the Smith's body and head – executing him.

Officer Smith – husband, father of two and police officer dies in that alley on that night.

The police funeral was an awesome sight. Coordinated by the Gotham City Police Department every member of service from Chief on down had a full-dress uniform with mourning bands across their badges, shiny shoes and white gloves. Officers from all over the nation came. Eulogies were given, bagpipes played Amazing Grace, a bugler offered up taps as a 21 gun salute was fired.

If you've never been to a police funeral they are impressive. But sadly they are too often preventable. Do I place the death of my hypothetical Officer Smith on the shoulders of his P.D. or his supervisors? No. However, in my

30 year career in law enforcement I have seen far too often the unfortunate and negative results of good but misapplied intentions. As they say, "The road to hell is paved with good intentions." "Gotham PD" bought into the "theory" espoused by far too many academicians that controlling an officer's use of force through restrictive policies is a good and proper thing. Training vendors looking to make a buck sold them on the concept of liability exposure by implementing a policy so rigid and convoluted that it takes its purveyor to explain it. By not training either their troops in use of force or their supervisors in use of force investigations they created mistrust and uncertainty in the minds of the officers they were promoted to protect.

Unreal you say? Perhaps *too real* I respond. As I write this the calendar year 2011 has ended. The numbers of officers killed in the line of duty were up again, the second year in a row.

Simplistic you say? The eternal realist and the 30 year police veteran in me responds that the scenario is all too possible based on agency paranoia about civil litigation and its driving force in policy, police training and supervision.

Good cops need their agencies to take care of them. They need to be trained in the legal parameters of use of force as well as the physical skills necessary to control violent suspects and protect their own lives. Good cops also need supervisors who are well trained in use of force investigations.

Critics of the police, theorists, academicians and micromanagers will say that I am an advocate of excessive use of force. That if agencies follow my recommendations it will lead to violations of citizen's constitutional rights, racism and police abuse. These same individuals will state that it is better to restrict officer's use of force more than what the law allows. They'll point to riots resulting from real and imagined police excesses as proof that it is better to restrict or limit officers than it is to allow them the full benefit of what the law allows.

Society expects officers to be "faster than a speeding bullet, more powerful than a locomotive and able to leap tall buildings with a single bound," to defy the law of physics ala *The Matrix* and to read a person's mind ascertaining their intent. An officer must respond with the reflexes of an Olympian, shoot like Annie Oakley and have the endurance of an Ironman competitor. They are expected to reason with the unreasonable and talk to the manic, depressed, mentally ill, emotionally disturbed and hyper-violent with equal aplomb. When assaulted with verbal insults, spit, punches or targeted with human urine or feces they must wipe it off with a smile and a deep understanding that it was the uniform that was targeted and not them personally. They cannot feel fear or anger and must wait for a suspect to fire first. When they fire back, they should shoot the gun out of the suspect's hand with one round. Their memories must be photographic and their written reports pieces of literature. When confronted with violence they must apply minimal levels of masterful non-injurious control like a Jedi Master.

And you know what? Most times they do.

But inside that blue polyester uniform is a human being, who despite his best intentions and training, is subject to the same human limitations and frailties as any other man on this Earth.

Until you've been in that uniform in that back alley alone with three suspects at zero-dark-thirty when the "fight is on" you really don't know what it means or what it's all about. Until such experience is earned, it's all theory and supposition.

Use of force is not "the fun part of police work" as the old police coffee mug portrayed. It is very scary, very real and the outcomes can be serious if not deadly for all involved.

> "Almost every use of force, however minute, poses some risk of death."
>
> Garrett v. Athens-Clarke County,
> 378 F. 3d 1274, 1280, n.12 (11th Cir. 2004)

Good men and women suit up every day in this country to patrol our streets, highways and communities. Their intentions are honorable and they are the best of the best and I am an unabashed supporter of them.

Let's train them, supervise them, support and defend them like the precious commodities they are.

Thanks for reading and remember to train like your life depends on it... because it does.

"May the Good Lord bless you with the strength and the will to train to win!"

KD
January, 2012

APPENDIX

Stone, Michael P., (1998). *"Taking the Fifth, Parts I, II, III and IV."* Lawyers, Training Bulletin

Brave, Michael, (1995). *"How Much Force is Reasonable?"* LAAW Int.

Hatch, David E. (2003*). "Officer-Involved Shootings and Use of Force."* CRC Press

Siddle, Bruce K. (1995). *"Sharpening the Warrior's Edge."* PPCT Research Publications

Artwohl, Alexis; Christensen, Loren W. (1997). *"Deadly Force Encounters."* Paladin Press

Goleman, Daniel (1995). *"Emotional Intelligence."* Bantam Trade Paperback

Artwohl, Alexis (2003). *"Deadly Force Encounters: Preparing to Survive, Coping with the Aftermath."*

National Institute of Justice (1999). *"Use of Force By Police: Overview of National and Local Data"*

U.S. Department of Justice; FBI (1997). *"In the Line of Fire: Violence Against Law Enforcement"*

Geller, William A.; Scott, Michael S. (1992) *"Deadly Force: What We Know."* Police Executive Research Forum

Wright, Doyle T. (2002) *"Officer Involved Shootings: Investigative Concepts and Issues."* PATC

Petrowski, Thomas D. (October/November, 2002) *"Use-of-Force Policies and Training A Reasoned Approach."* F.B.I. Bulletin

Patrick, Urey W.; Hall, John C. (2005) *"In Defense of Self and Others... Issues, Facts & Fallacies – the Realities of Law Enforcement's Use of Deadly Force."* Carolina Academic Press

Ryan, Jack (2010) *"The Law and Best Practices of Successful Police Operations – second edition"* Liability Risk Management Institute

Ross, Darrell L.; Chan, Theodore C. (2006) *"Sudden Deaths in Custody."* Humana Press

Klinger, David (2004) *"Into the Kill Zone."* Jossey-Bass

Di Maio, Theresa; Di Maio, Vincent J.M. (2006) *"Excited Delirium Syndrome: Cause of Death and Prevention."* CRC Press

Bostain, John (Fall, 2006) *"Use of Force: Are Continuums Still Necessary?"*; FLETC Journal

Chabris, Christopher; Simons, Daniel (2009) *"The Invisible Gorilla: How Our Intuitions Deceive Us."* Broadway Paperbacks

Sapolsky, Robert M. (2004) *"Why Zebras Don't Get Ulcers: The Acclaimed Guide to Stress, Stress-Related Diseases, and Coping – Third Edition"* Owl Books

Williams, George T. (2006) *"Force Reporting for Every Cop."* Jones and Bartlett

Aitchison, Will (2004) *"The Rights of Law Enforcement Officers – 5th Edition."* Labor Relations Information System

Rahtz, Howard (2003) *"Understanding Police Use of Force."* Criminal Justice Press

Jorg, R. Blaine (2006) *"13 Minutes."* Self-Published

Ross, Darrell L. (2003) "Civil *Liability in Criminal Justice – third edition"* Anderson

Skolnick, Jerome H.; Fyfe, James J. (1993) *"Above the Law: Police and the Excessive Use of Force."* Free Press

Webb, Howard (2011) *"Managing the Use of Force Incident."* Charles C. Thomas

Made in the USA
Lexington, KY
21 January 2013